ANOTHER DAY'S
JOURNEY

Black
Churches
Confronting
the
American
Crisis

Robert M. Franklin

FORTRESS PRESS   MINNEAPOLIS

ANOTHER DAY'S JOURNEY
Black Churches Confronting the American Crisis

Cover design: Brad Norr Design
Text design: David Lott
Cover art: "The migration gained in momentum." Panel 18 from *The Migration Series* by Jacob Lawrence. (1940–41; text and title revised by the artist, 1993.) Photograph © 1997 The Museum of Modern Art, New York. Used by permission.
Author photo: Bud Smith Photo ©

Library of Congress Cataloging-in-Publication Data

Franklin, Robert Michael, 1954–
    Another day's journey : Black churches confronting the American crisis / Robert M. Franklin.
       p.   cm.
    Includes bibliographical references and index.
    ISBN 0-8006-3096-3 (alk. paper)
    1. Afro-American churches. 2. Church work with Afro-American youth. 3. Church work with Afro-Americans. I. Title.
BR563.N4F69 1997
277.3'0829'08996073—dc21   97-37342
                                          CIP

American National Standard for Information Sciences—Permanence of Paper for Printed Library Materials, ANSI Z329.48-1984.

Manufactured in the U.S.A.   AF 1-3096

01   00   99   98   97   1   2   3   4   5   6   7   8   9   10

*In memory of great and eternal souls
who sacrificed themselves for the common good.
They have journeyed to a better country.*

Dr. Samuel DeWitt Proctor

Dr. Mac Charles Jones

Dr. James Melvin Washington

Dr. Betty Shabazz

Bishop Louis Henry Ford

93516

CONTENTS

PREFACE

This book was written on the run. Well, almost. The process actually began four years ago with research on changes and continuity in African American churches since the civil rights movement. The research was supported by the Lilly Endowment, and my labors were guided and assisted by two exceptional graduate students who have since become accomplished professionals. Dr. Rosetta Ross teaches ethics at the Interdenominational Theological Center in Atlanta, and Rev. Terry Walker is a development executive there. After joining the staff of the Ford Foundation, I thought that I would never get around to writing this text. But friends at the Candler School of Theology, the Ford Foundation, and ITC urged me to complete the work before assuming the ITC presidency. This meant writing on the airplane, in New York City restaurants, and in Atlanta libraries.

I must mention my indebtedness to Lynn Huntley, Alison Bernstein, Robert Curvin, Melvin Oliver, and James Joseph, friends in the foundation community who challenged and sharpened my thinking about many of the issues treated in the book. I am grateful to Karen Smith, Richard Adams, and Svanhild Vage, who assisted me in New York. Also, I am deeply grateful for the help of Dr. Emmanuel McCall, Bishop Roy L. Winbush, Bishop John Hurst Adams, Dr. James H. Costen, and Elizabeth Littlejohn at ITC. I am also grateful for the moral support of Kevin LaGree, the dean at Candler, and to Candler's entire faculty; Dorcas Doward, the program assistant in the Black Church Studies program; Ira and Cynthia Moreland, who unselfishly covered my carpooling responsibilities while I was away; and all of the good people who helped care for our children during this strenuous time including my beloved sister Cheri Rachelle, Catherine Underwood, Anika Walker, and my cousin, Sonya Gordon, and especially my mother, "Dot" Franklin. They ensured that I had the necessary time and resources to complete the manuscript.

Writing a book can be a heavy load to inflict on a family. I must thank my generous and devoted wife, Cheryl, for reading the entire manuscript even when she was exhausted from her Ob-Gyn practice. The nights I found her sleeping with the manuscript in her arms humbled, but did not discourage, me. Cheryl and I are grateful to her colleagues at the Meridian Medical Group for supporting her as she has supported me during my years of commuting weekly between New York and Atlanta, and now in the strenuous demands placed on a seminary president's family. I am grateful for the patience and understanding of my children, Imani, Robert III, and Julian, and for the support of our extended families.

I express gratitude for a terrific editor, J. Michael West, a wordsmith with whom I first became acquainted while at Harvard Divinity School. We worked together on my first book, *Liberating Visions* (1990), and now I see how important an imaginative editor can be. Also, the good people at Fortress Press have been very supportive and creative in moving this book from idea to reality in a short span of time. A special word of appreciation goes to David Lott and Brad Norr for their design talents and to John Turnbull for copyediting the manuscript. A dear friend, Francelle Calhoun, also proofread and offered suggestions for improving the book.

I have written this book with the hope that it will help to connect communities that I care a great deal about—the church, the academy, the nonprofit sector, youth organizations, and organized philanthropy. I hope that it will prove useful for stimulating much-needed dialogue across sectors and disciplines. If we are to solve the problems that plague our communities, we must begin to work with new and unlikely partners. As Booker T. Washington would say, we must do common things in an uncommon manner. Business as usual will not suffice for the journey ahead.

Recall the words of Mahatma Gandhi: "We must be the change that we seek."

1 BEGINNINGS

The Making of a Public Theologian

I t was April 4, 1968, on the far South-side of Chicago. I was a fourteen-year-old freshman on my way home from Morgan Park High School when a black driver passing by shouted out his window, "Dr. King has been shot. All hell is gonna break loose." Although I was halfway home, I decided to return to school to see how the school community would respond to this awful news. Even before I made it to school, what I saw convinced me that the city was in for a long and difficult night. The street was transformed into a stage on which a confusing and violent drama was unfolding. Young African Americans were running along the street hurling rocks and insults at white bus drivers and passengers in automobiles. White youth were reciprocating these gestures. Soon I could hear store windows shattering nearby and, in the distance, see billows of smoke from burning buildings.

When I finally arrived home, I saw television reports that showed urban America on fire. It seemed such an inappropriate response to the death of an advocate of nonviolence. There had been no similar response when Malcolm X was killed three years earlier. Yet Malcolm had been a bold advocate of using violent means to repel enemies. Malcolm had even been photographed dressed in a business suit and holding a rifle. Thereby he had become the icon of black militancy in the 1960s.

The long night passed slowly and found my family awake until 3:00 A.M., watching television, praying, and silently pondering the future. The morning after was eerie. My neighborhood of black working-class people seemed to be waiting to inhale, as the wind had been knocked from their chests the night before. Everyone I met seemed to be caught between grief and rage. We all knew that the world would never be the same. One of the black community's best examples of moral citizenship had been felled in the line of duty, leaving the rest of us to consider how committed we would be to Dr. King's vision and agenda. The world of my immediate neighborhood grew closer during the days and weeks that followed his assassination. Neighbors lingered in front of their homes to discuss the state of the nation and of the African American quest for full participation in the larger society. When the family sat together to watch the funeral on television, for the first time I saw the campus of Morehouse College, where Dr. King had matriculated, and its president, Dr. Benjamin Mays. Watching faculty and other dignitaries march in procession across the campus, I felt deeply drawn to it. It seemed to symbolize the excellence, dignity, and nobility that King had come to represent.

A Safe Place

I was reared in a household with a large extended family including my grandmother Martha McCann, two grown uncles, one aunt, my mother and father, and three younger siblings. Next door lived my great aunt along with several of her grown children. Since all of these folks had migrated to Chicago from rural Mississippi during the Depression, it felt as if we lived in our own Southern compound tucked inside the big city. When we entered the extended family compound, we felt that we were in the safest place on earth, a place where all sorts of goods and services were shared, where no one went hungry, where everyone knew our name, and where we all encouraged one another to face another day. It was this sense of deep security provided by so many working-class and poor black families that kept black youths from realizing that we were poor, if measured by the standards of the government or the sociologists a few miles away at the University of Chicago.

Because this compound and others like it were so important to my own development and to many other African Americans who have found success in the era after the civil rights movement, it is worth describing its characteristics a bit more. Although families today may not be able to re-create entirely such close-knit bonds, we can all draw guidance and inspiration from the successful adaptive strategies that these wise elders have passed on to us.

Martha McCann was the beloved matriarch of our family system. Every day she and her sister prepared enormous meals to feed the army of working family members who would converge on the households after work. Mealtime was always fun for us because we could listen to the adult talk while consuming prodigious portions of fried chicken, corn bread, collard greens, and candied yams, which were washed down with tall glasses of fresh lemonade and topped off with sweet-potato pie, peach cobbler, and homemade ice cream. My grandmother, like so many grandmothers from other cultures, had a wonderful way of showing care. She would feed people until they were barely able to walk. A meal wasn't a success unless people fell into a deep, relaxing stupor afterward.

Grandma could also stop a riot. I once watched her walk into the middle of two street gangs that were about to come to blows. She spoke to them about the love of God and how they should not throw their lives away in violence, and how each boy would break the heart of his mother if he were to be fatally wounded. Amazingly, the young brothers smiled at her and walked away, certain to fight another day. But through her stunning and risky street interventions I learned something important about conflict resolution. By placing one's life on the line, one claims a posture of moral authority to speak truth to all kinds of power. Sometimes those words can redirect hate. Those words can become power.

Of course, in those days, hurting a woman was stigmatized as unmanly, as a breach of the honor code of masculinity. Today, changes have occurred that might render Grandma's actions nearly suicidal. The code has eroded and civil society, wherein citizens take responsibility for the hygiene of their streets, has declined with it. But even amid that decline we have seen numerous instances in which community members, especially mothers who have lost children to street violence, have organized and mobilized out of pain and fear to recapture their living spaces and to resist the encroachments of social evil.

> By placing one's life on the line, one claims a posture of moral authority to speak truth to all kinds of power. Sometimes those words can redirect hate. Those words can become power.

People throughout the old neighborhood, especially my friends and my uncle's drinking buddies, knew when to drop by to partake of my grandmother's culinary arts. And, because she was the head of the mothers' board at church, lots of church ladies in starched white dresses were around the house. This made for fascinating chemistry, to see the winos and the sisters of the mothers' board dining under the same roof, from the same menu. All were welcome here. In fact, my grandmother's table seemed more inclusive than our local congregation, where the male clergy held power and status, the licensed women also held status, and the sinners ranked at the bottom.

Occasionally, the "saints" and "sinners" got into heated discussions about the Bible, personal morality, and justice in society. I always learned a lot from these wide-ranging talks. My grandmother understood her role to be that of the moderator who ensured that everyone remained civil and respectful. Uncle Dudley's stories were always spellbinding and funny. The kids didn't know that he was making up most of the material. We especially liked his street adventure stories; he was a Chicago cop who had been around a lot of dead people. He'd spin a story about walking into a room filled with corpses after a particularly violent Chicago weekend, and one of the corpses would bolt upward and begin speaking. Grandma would scold him for lying and terrifying the children, but we loved that stuff and never got enough.

Grandma's house and her table were places where the community met, and where good religion was practiced and experienced. Grandma's garden next door was a place of many treasures. I remember long, hot summer days when she would spend hours turning over the soil and tending crops of collard and spinach greens, tomatoes, and golden stalks of corn. From this small garden, her ministry extended throughout the neighborhood and far out into the city. She sent fresh vegetables to poorer families in the neighborhood. She cooked large pots of greens and had my mother drive her to sick and shut-in church members who needed a good meal. My brother and I were no more than six years old, but we watched her strange behavior and marveled.

> Grandma's garden represented defiance, self-empowerment, practical enrichment, and hope for the larger community.

It is now clear to me that Grandma was resisting the dehumanizing effects of urban living. Having moved to Chicago, she discovered black people who owned no land, lived in tiny apartments, and ate canned food. This was different from what they had known in the South, where, despite their impoverished condition, they were attached to the land and could feed their families. Migration seemed to be an act of voluntary disenfranchisement. At another level, however, it represented empowerment by seizing the opportunity to earn higher wages for their hard work. Her garden represented defiance, self-empowerment, practical enrichment, and hope for the larger community.

Cultivating Religion

When Grandma left her garden, it was usually to get dressed for church. The same woman who wore the straw hat and plaid, cotton dresses would rapidly transform into Mother Martha McCann, clad in her starched white uniform and hat. At church she would lead the midweek worship services with prayer, songs, and testimonies of God's goodness to the saints. The younger and ambitious pastor, Elder Louis H. Ford, depended on her and her colleagues to sustain the congregation while he worked on finding new members and new resources to support his vision of building a grand sanctuary for the people of God. Mother McCann accepted that part of her calling was to nurture the congregation by ministering to the body and soul.

Although we were part of a Pentecostal tradition that did not think very highly of formal education, I was fortunate to have a pastor who supported academic excellence and a family that rewarded performance. I recall visiting preachers who would declare that studying was a waste of time for people who knew the Lord and could read the Bible. Depending on the age and status of the preacher, Pastor Ford would either keep silent or refute the remarks. One day after a preacher had held forth on how he had never gone to school beyond fifth grade yet had been successful as a pastor, Pastor Ford simply asked the congregation whether they would seek a trained physician or any well-intentioned Christian if they needed brain surgery. The point registered.

Although the prospect of attending the formal worship service was not much fun for us as kids, we did enjoy what preceded it. Before worship began, all of the young people were invited to participate in the "Breakfast Club." This was a seventy-five-minute forum in which breakfast was served and various academic and social skill-building exercises were conducted. The pastor, who by then had become a bishop, loved presiding at these weekly sessions in which prizes were awarded to the young person who had memorized the most Bible verses, who could interpret a verse persuasively, or who could identify great moments from black history. The most dreaded practice was being called on to expound extemporaneously on the current events of the week.

It was amazing to witness: a room crammed with a hundred kids, many of them from the nearby Robert Taylor Homes (the nation's largest low-income public housing complex), competing intellectually and having their characters shaped by hard-working Southern migrants. Occasionally we would be exposed to guest speakers from different professions. Bishop Ford enjoyed showing us off to Mayor Richard J. Daley and other politicians who dropped in to pay him a visit.

We were also taught etiquette and manners, and the boys were taught to be chivalrous. We were helped to role play reactions to people who might disrespect us. Without realizing it, we received a version of the citizenship education given to civil rights demonstrators throughout the South. Bishop Ford believed that it was particularly important for young black men to learn constructive ways of expressing their anger. "Don't let your anger be your weakness. You don't have to stop what you're doing and fight every racist who comes along to bother you," he would exhort. "Outsmart him by finishing what you're doing, then pick the right moment to deal with the situation."

The bishop would complete our success training by taking groups to the golf course. There we learned to caddy and, he hoped, to love the game. More important, we learned that in places like the golf course important business deals and hiring decisions were made. We saw famous people like the boxer Joe Louis and the singer Sam Cooke. Although the bishop's appearance on golf courses with secular personalities was controversial, he clearly enjoyed that he was mentoring a future generation of civic leaders. In this respect, he practiced at the level of the local church what Booker T. Washington, the president of Tuskegee Institute, did nationally. Both sought to cultivate in a caring, patient manner virtues and behaviors that would promote individual and collective betterment. Washington referred to his message as a "gospel of the hand, head, and heart."

It is also noteworthy that these breakfast meetings took place in Chicago's oldest building, the Widow Clarke House, an elegant white mansion that had survived the Chicago fire of 1871, but had been left in disrepair only to be purchased, renovated, and maintained by the St. Paul Church of God in Christ. The pastor, our own Bishop Ford, capitalized brilliantly on the fact that this historical monument was being maintained by a black Pentecostal congregation. He invited all sorts of dignitaries to the grounds for tours, and presented it as a public space that had been cared for by the religious faithful. This was only one small part of Ford's expansive public vision. Since that time, the house has been sold to the city, moved, and is on display in a historic district near downtown.

Today my Breakfast Club companions are scattered around the country and have become physicians, lawyers, entrepreneurs, ministers, journalists, and teachers. In view of the remarkable effect that one pastor at one local church had on scores of youth, it behooves congregations today to consider instituting programs that can make a measurable difference. Such programs do not cost much money, nor do they require lots of time from one individual. Churches and clergy that do not have something like the breakfast program ought to be challenged to institute one immediately, or to explain why they have not.

Education, Chicago-Style

Chicago during the 1960s was a dangerous place for a black male teenager. At that time Chicago enjoyed the distinction of having the largest and best-organized street gangs in the nation. The largest and most notorious was the Blackstone Rangers. In subsequent years, it was known variously as the P-Stone Nation and the El-Rukns. During a routine week at school, we would hear stories about a classmate being stabbed, robbed, or shot by a Ranger for entering an off-limits neighborhood or for trying to date one of "their" women.

Chicago was already segregated along ethnic and racial lines, so it seemed particularly absurd to further divide the black community into gang-controlled turfs. Nevertheless, turf wars often broke out, and we learned to run for cover or to stay low on the ground when a gang account was settled violently. The far South Side of the city was "controlled" and patrolled by a smaller rival gang known as the Disciples or Gangster Disciples. Our general affinity as unaffiliated kids was with the Disciples, who were not known for terrorizing innocent people.

Recognizing that both gangs and religious communities have their own sacred spaces, times, rituals, gestures, vestments, symbols, secrets, and financial strategies, scholars have offered comparisons between them. The Blackstone Rangers wore red bandanas while the Disciples wore blue. Recognizing the colors was important for the nonaligned since one might be asked without notice whose colors they were. More intimidating was the necessity of being able to "represent" on demand. That is, anyone could be ordered by a gang member to display or enact the identifying gestures of the respective group. Functionally, this resembled making the sign of the cross, except that it usually involved striking one's chest with one's fist and ending with a salute, such as placing three fingers across the heart (a pitchfork).

> *Both gangs and religious communities have their own sacred spaces, times, rituals, gestures, vestments, symbols, secrets, and financial strategies.*

As if all of this activity weren't challenging enough, the Rangers began to draft new, uninterested, and unwilling members into the gang. Walking to school became highly charged, because one could be stopped by a car filled with gang members, forced to register one's name and other pertinent information, and to pay a small sum of money, and ordered to wear the colors of the gang and to report for a meeting at a designated place and time. Two of my friends were accosted in this way. One of them refused to comply with the many demands. Days later, his father's car was spray-painted with gang insignia. My parents considered this situation and pondered how to keep me from becoming a high school gangster or victim.

On top of the academic work occupying me and most of my friends, these life-threatening overtures created an additional set of adolescent burdens. We see a similar and, perhaps more intense, version of this in many communities today. Those who care about the prospects of inner-city youths should try to empathize with the fragility and complexity of the learning enterprise that many of them face. We were young, gifted, and black and did not disdain academic excellence. Indeed, friends like Mae Jemison, who later became the nation's first black female astronaut, embodied our desire for intellectual achievement. Still, our academic success went against the grain of the environment in which we lived.

Those who care about the prospects of inner-city youths should try to empathize with the fragility and complexity of the learning enterprise that many of them face.

During the same period, black consciousness was rising. Students listened to the speeches of Malcolm X and began to wear their hair in "natural" or "Afro" style and to identify with other blacks in a new way. A part of the awful legacy of slavery preserved by many of our ancestors was the mistrust of others in the competition to earn the good will of the master. Malcolm, more than any other contemporary leader, sought to demolish these practices and to instill more cooperative, trusting working relationships throughout the black community in the United States and abroad.

After Dr. King's murder, the Black Panther Party in Chicago became a high-profile and, to many young blacks, attractive way to embrace the black nationalism of which Malcolm and others spoke. For teenagers like me, who began the journey to school each morning dreading that the Rangers or Disciples might rudely interrupt our lives forever, the Panthers provided a fascinating alternative. Most of my peers were enthralled by the radical chic of the Panthers. The Panthers inspired us to dress in black leather jackets and berets, and to quote Thomas Jefferson and Che Guevara. The

Panthers helped to reinforce the point that we could be well read, articulate, and cool.

When the Democratic National Convention came to Chicago in 1968, the city seemed charged with anxiety and excitement. I begged my parents to let me join the protesters downtown. No way. Instead, I made my father sit and listen to recorded speeches of Eldridge Cleaver, whose language was so foul that my father suggested that people of his generation might be more persuaded by the substance of the argument if the manner in which it was expressed were more dignified.

For many people, the convention will always be remembered for the chaos in the streets, the police riot, and Mayor Daley's heavy-handedness toward demonstrators. But for me the most lasting image would be State Representative Julian Bond of Georgia being nominated vice president of the United States, which he had to decline because of his young age. Bond was a person who expressed himself with enormous dignity and persuasive power. As news profiles focused on Bond's background, once again Morehouse College came into view. I began to read more about Bond and Morehouse and soon began to feel a tug toward this place far away from home.

Joys and Terrors

Anyone who remembers the joyful and terrifying years of adolescence will understand when I say that I was a person of many faces, driven by conflicting voices and visions. I was the church kid whose formative years were spent in Sunday school, the youth choir, vacation Bible school, and so on. I was also the young aggressive male crash-landing into puberty and clumsily trying to establish my romantic macho identity, an endeavor widely ignored by young women throughout the neighborhood. In addition, I was a budding politician intrigued by the gloss and slime of modern politics and public service. I was also awakening intellectually to the vast world of ideas stored in books. Bishop Ford used to say that the best way to hide something from most people would be to place it in a book. And although my parents had made what they considered to be an investment and a sacrifice in purchasing encyclopedias, it wasn't really cool to be smart and widely read until the Panthers came on the scene exposing us to Marx and Hegel. Then, being smart was not just acceptable, it became sexy. For me, the church, the street, and the academy were slowly fusing in a new synthesis that lacked a single guiding model.

> *It wasn't really cool to be smart and widely read until the Panthers came on the scene exposing us to Marx and Hegel. Then, being smart was not just acceptable, it became sexy.*

The worst day of my young life came when I was expelled from school and fired from my part-time job within a matter of hours. It would be my first lesson in experiencing both tragedy and the redemptive love of God. Although I was too young to join the Panthers, I was a wannabe who hung around them when it was safe and convenient. I knew that if I went too far, my father would apply the force of his quiet and rarely exercised discipline. It is ironic and revealing that the adolescent militant who flirted with gang activity and felt so powerful and independent still respected the symbolic power of his father. I feared my mother and extended family's sanctions as well, but somehow the bond with my father provided a stronger and somewhat mysterious check on my behavior. I do not fully understand the dynamics of this link, but it does underscore the importance of fathers investing in child development.

While at school one afternoon, a few older nonstudents, whom we assumed to be Panthers, were nearby trying to sell copies of the group's paper. They seemed generally unhappy about something. Later we learned that one of the group's revered leaders, Fred Hampton, had been killed when Chicago police raided his home. The Panthers urged all black students to walk out and demonstrate. Since they couldn't enter the school building, they sought sympathizers in the student body. There were three of us who sympathized, and one of my associates allegedly pulled a fire alarm. We weren't together when it occurred, though he later gleefully took credit for the mischief. As everyone filed out into the street, the Panthers urged black students not to reenter. I supported the walkout, and the day ended with a lot of angry speechmaking that had no concrete agenda apart from an invitation to support the next rally and to donate money to free Huey Newton, the group's imprisoned leader.

The next day while I was sitting on campus during a study break, a large police officer walked up and told me to follow him. He ushered me into the office of the vice principal, who informed me that I was being expelled from school for participating in the previous day's walkout. He accused me of other offenses in which I was not involved, and it became apparent that he was building a case that would keep me away for a long time. "Get your things and leave immediately," were the last words I heard.

I held a part-time job at the Jewel's food-store chain, not far from my house. I was employed as a produce clerk. This was considered to be status position; it entailed a large measure of trust and autonomy. I weighed and marked the prices on vegetables and fruit, and I was responsible for presenting them on the shelves in an attractive way. This after-school employment was important for occupying my evening hours constructively and for contributing to my sense of being a responsible, productive person.

That day, I went straight to work after school. Contemplating how best to break the bad news to my parents, a peace offering came into view. I would offer my folks a wonderful fruit basket and then apologetically tell them about the recent unpleasantries. I handpicked the most luscious and perfect fruit available, reduced the price significantly so that I could easily pay for it, had it stamped "paid," and placed it on the service counter where employees' purchases were kept until closing time.

Just as the store was closing, the manager Ken Dean approached and quietly asked me to follow him. When we walked over to the counter, he had my bag open and asked, "What is this?" I fumbled for words, explaining that it was a gift and that I had discounted it. "Why don't you get your things. That's it, I'm sorry." Twice in one day I had been kicked out of a place where I belonged.

Walking home that night, I felt what John of the Cross called the dark night of the soul. How could this have happened so suddenly? Was there a purpose behind it all? Was I a bad person? How could I be so stupid?

My parents and grandmother were grace for me that night. I expected the worst, and I deserved a raw reception. But they listened and forgave and helped me think through a plan for returning to school. Sometimes people can be the grace and love of God. And, if you remember the story of the prodigal son, there are moments in all of our lives when we need grace and love to bring us home. There are children drifting far from their parents' love and good upbringing right now. Their journeys into self-destruction, despair, and alienation will have to run their course. But all of us can be ready to become the grace and love of God in times of trouble.

> *There are children drifting far from their parents' love and good upbringing right now. Their journeys into self-destruction, despair, and alienation will have to run their course. But all of us can become the grace and love of God in times of trouble.*

I returned to school with the determination of a bull. I read everything I could get my hands on in the library. After reading Plato's *Republic*, I wrote an essay about taking risks to understand people who are different; the essay was published in the school paper. Teachers began to recommend that I be transferred into honors-level classes. Other teachers who had known me earlier expressed disbelief on hearing that I was becoming a serious student. My teacher, Mrs. Evison, and counselor, Mrs. Carmichael, defended me and urged other teachers to give students a chance to change. At graduation I received the Citizenship Award.

Beyond Parochialisms

One day my father surprised me by saying that he had wanted to attend Morehouse when he was younger and that he really wanted me to go there. He was proud of my recovery from the storms of the previous year. Dad hadn't been able to attend Morehouse because he was drafted into the army, and after the Korean War had started his family. We hadn't talked much about college before, so this came as a wonderful bolt of good news.

Months later, my mother and I were aboard a Greyhound bus, bound for the red clay of Georgia, leaving behind St. Paul Church of God in Christ, Esmond Elementary School, Morgan Park High School, the Blackstone Rangers, Black Panthers, Jewel's Food Store, and many other places that I'll always remember. Nineteen hours later, we were met by Bishop Husband, who took us to the famed Paschal Hotel in Atlanta. The next morning, we took a taxi to the campus, and I took my place in the long registration line. Dressed in a shirt and tie, with a new briefcase in my hands, I waved good-bye to Mom, aware that I wouldn't see her for several months.

Later I learned from my cousin, Rev. Walter Battle, that she returned and called him, crying over the phone about having taken and left her child in a Georgia school. He consoled her by reminding her that hundreds of other mothers that night were taking their sons to prison or to the cemetery. On reflection, her countenance lifted.

Morehouse was easy to love and easy to hate. The first day, the staff began to instill the Morehouse mystique. We sat in chapel and were reminded of the luminaries who had gone before us. We were told that we were leaders and that we should always conduct ourselves as if all of the nation were watching. We were told to look to our left and to our right and note that two of the guys around us would not be there at graduation time. True.

Although a surprising number of guys had no interest in things academic or political, those who were serious had a great time making friendships with the most talented young men that black America had to offer. Still I felt restless and was tugged by the unsettling sense that I was too parochial to be the kind of world citizen called for by Dr. King.

Morehouse pushed us beyond our parochialism. My professors were urbane and cosmopolitan. Robert Brisbane, who taught political science, was known to quote Aristotle while fingering his Phi Beta Kappa key. But he also shared personal memories about the Harlem Renaissance and told stories about how Dr. King hadn't been that great a student, which always encouraged us. E. Edward Jones taught French but, while discussing the varieties of Negritude in Afro-French literature, also taught us to tie our own bow ties. E. B. Williams, an economics professor, told us to prepare for an interview with a graduate school or corporate recruiter by consuming the contents of the morning's *Wall Street Journal;* he recommended citing its contents subtly during the interview. The president of the college, Dr. Hugh Gloster, pushed us in his weekly remarks to distinguish ourselves in the larger arena of life, and not to be content with being good black lawyers, doctors, or scholars.

Thanks to these influences, I found myself applying for and being awarded an overseas scholarship for a year of study in England. In the fall of 1973, all the members of the family compound drove in caravan to O'Hare Airport, where I was placed on a British Airways jet for London. Sadly, my grandmother had died one month earlier. She would have wanted to be there that day. She would have smiled and thanked God to see one of her offspring launching out into a bigger world. A woman who had never completed elementary school and had reared ten children alone in the big city was making her vision felt in the world. But, then, she was there that day.

Journeys Abroad and Within

Culture shock: I was transplanted from the Southside of Chicago and the halls of Morehouse to a small British town surrounding a cathedral eight hundred years old. Durham University was comprised of thirteen colleges, all different in character. I was a member of Van Mildert College, a modern, attractive campus on the outskirts of the university.

Walking into town, one passed sheep grazing in the fields and could see the small Palatine river winding around the cathedral and through town. I enjoyed worshiping at St. Margaret's Anglican

Church, a small church in town that nurtured my appreciation for Western liturgical practices. Groups of parish members and students visited a nearby mental hospital each week. I was asked to come along and grew to enjoy the opportunity to bring some happiness into the lives of the patients. I still remember one patient, Malcolm, a burly guy who frightened most people away. But he was intrigued by me, thinking that I was an Indian from America. He had read about and watched televised versions of American Indians, enough to be partially informed and quite confused. Each week he'd ask me to relate how my people had demolished General Custer's army. He'd get a great kick out of this, and would laugh so hard that he'd fall off his chair. He didn't care much for Custer.

I attended a weekly Bible study conducted by students at Van Mildert. Students Graham Thornton and Clive Taylor introduced me to the writings of C. S. Lewis. Lewis's book *Mere Christianity* helped me think through my identity as a Christian systematically. One evening during the prayer time for our Bible study, something unusual happened. Clive began to speak and pray in tongues. I was shocked. I had grown up in a Pentecostal church where speaking in tongues was common, although I had not done so. I thought that this was the sort of exotic religiosity to which oppressed people enjoyed exclusive access. I didn't know that white people, much less the rather staid British, could or would indulge. Then, to my utter amazement, a few minutes later another student interpreted the earlier utterance. The interpretation had to do with God's desire that the prayer group not be so insular and that we become a more public entity in the university. All of this was blowing my mind.

The tongues incident set off a small storm of controversy among the Bible study members. Was this a legitimate spiritual expression? Should everyone seek to speak in tongues? Why were strange tongues necessary at all if God could give an interpretation that would be understood by everyone? We had some painful and fascinating discussions in the weeks that followed and almost came apart as a group. But the two student leaders, Graham (not Pentecostal and skeptical) and Clive (newly charismatic but undogmatic), sought to remain in partnership. This incident reminded me of the tensions which divided all sorts of black, white, and Latino churches in the United States. Many of the churches had split over this issue. The students in England provided me with a dramatic example of unity without uniformity. Love provides the courage to tolerate and accept what one does not fully understand, until better insight comes.

> *Love provides the courage to tolerate and accept what one does not fully understand, until better insight comes.*

Despite my Pentecostal upbringing with its annual tent-revival rituals and obligatory recommitments to Christ, I was skeptical of nonrational spiritual expressions. So I was not fully prepared for an occurrence during early morning prayer several months after the prayer group experience. As I prepared to go to church, while washing my face and meditating about something, I felt a churning in my spirit. Compelled to move my somewhat diffuse meditation into more focused, explicit prayer, I began asking for illumination. In the midst of what felt like a movement into new levels of communion with God, I groaned and uttered sounds that were nonsense to my cognitive faculties, which were simultaneously working very hard to monitor and analyze this leap into the unknown. It made me recall the apostle Paul's observations in Romans 8 regarding the inadequacy of language in moments of deep emotional prayer. After a few seconds, I stopped and prayed for insight. None came immediately. What did occur soon thereafter was a reorienting of my worldview and self-understanding.

I began to pay more attention to the way that powerful emotions attach to religious causes and drive people to extraordinary behavior, some of it noble and honorable, some of it mad and evil. It became largely an intellectual quest. I did not become a better or more moral person instantly. I did become more introspective and attentive to the motives that underlie my behavior. This intense prayer centered my perspective on life so that I became more respectful of the nonrational, emotional dimensions of human existence. I began to look at everything from the perspectives of reason and emotion, seeking to keep the two in dialogue to produce a richer appreciation for the density of human experience. My encounter with the Spirit helped me realize that God has bestowed on humans the gifts of reason and spiritual illumination so that we do not become one-dimensional creatures. Reason and revelation must ever be dialogue partners. This is part of what it means to be created in the image of God.

My encounter with the Spirit helped me to realize that God has bestowed on humans the gifts of reason and spiritual illumination so that we do not become one-dimensional creatures.

During the year abroad, I visited fascinating places in Scotland, Wales, Spain, Morocco, and the Soviet Union, most of them with my closest friend, Asa Yancey, Jr. I had read the autobiographies of Du Bois, King, Malcolm X, and others who noted the importance of travel to their personal and intellectual development. Far from a luxury, I believe that travel is a moral imperative for those who seek to lead people. As the Ghanaian proverb warns, "Do not claim that your mother's stew is the best in the world if you have never left your village."

Lou Rawls's song about the hawk has aggrandized Chicago's legendary windiness. But England combined bone-chilling cold with bone-penetrating dampness. All year long I wore the leather coat my extended family had given to me. So, when the Christmas break arrived, it was axiomatic that I would head as far south as my modest budget would allow. The destination was Casablanca, Morocco—in my mind, a place of warmth, mystery, and romance. To get there, I had to travel via charter plane from London to Barcelona, then by train to southern Spain, where I would take a boat to North Africa. I thought that if I could brave the Chicago el trains and buses in the winter, I could manage this trip.

My reading for the journey included two classic travel novels: *On the Road* by Jack Kerouac and *Down and Out in Paris and London* by George Orwell. Both texts helped me to endure the manifold inconveniences and to embrace the magic of traveling to unimaginable places. Barcelona was a city of wide, tree-lined boulevards, breathtaking seafood, and friendly people. The farther south I traveled, the darker the people became. Racial mixing seemed to be determined by latitude. Southern Spain was rich with Moorish architecture, culturally complex foods, and attractive people.

It took nearly two weeks to reach Torremolinos, where I boarded a large ferry en route to Morocco. The passage across the Mediterranean was turbulent, and I was sick most of the time. But words cannot express the feeling I had when the coast of Africa came into view. I thought for a moment about the millions of Africans who had left the continent headed west. My eyes scanned the sea waters for the remains of those who had committed suicide by jumping into shark-infested waters. Now I was going home.

My goal was to spend New Year's Eve in Casablanca. By the time I reached Casablanca I had nearly run out of money, so I was unable to eat much. I spent the days strolling the streets, peeking into mosques, and consuming bread, cheese, water, sweet wine, and strong coffee, which were all I could afford. I had learned from George Orwell that it was helpful to eat a pungent cheese, so that hours after consuming it the aftertaste gave one the impression of having recently dined.

Seeing devout Muslims interrupt their business practices to pray during the day was very impressive and humbling. My spirituality felt shallow compared to theirs. I found myself wanting to read more about religious belief systems throughout the world. Suddenly my passion for political science and pre-law studies was waning. I began to ask a new and different kind of question; namely, what is the ultimate purpose of human existence?

When New Year's Eve rolled around, I sat on the curb in a large public square in the city and attempted to consume my meal, which consisted of bread, a can of peanut butter from Senegal, and a soda. I encountered one small problem. I realized that I had no can opener. I improvised and smashed open the can on the side of a curb. Like a prodigal son, I thought, I'm a long way from Grandma's dinner table. Despite the modest meal, when the ships in the harbor sounded their New Year's bells and horns, I was perfectly at peace with the world.

A few months later my overseas journey came to an end with a two-week tour of the Soviet Union. I visited the picturesque city of Leningrad (now St. Petersburg), Moscow, and Sochi, located on the Black Sea. During my tour in Sochi, I was befriended by a brilliant and beautiful Asian woman who was a medical student and a member of the Communist Party. She spoke enough English for us to have good conversations about the mentality and aspirations of Soviet youths. She was quite intrigued with American popular culture. At one point, I tried to interpret the meaning of Jimi Hendrix's song "Purple Haze" to the amusement of a group of Russian and Polish students. During our talks, she noted that young people no longer believed in God, which in Russian is known as *Bog*. Faith was a relic of the old order which had been eradicated by scientific socialism. Preparing to leave Sochi, I noticed that the local stores were stocking American flags in preparation for the arrival of President Richard Nixon.

I departed Russia with an unsettled sense that something powerful in the human psyche was being suppressed and denied in the culture. Could a government wipe out the faith of millions of people? Why was the death of God so important to the future of communism?

Theological Bearings

I returned to the United States with these and similar questions swirling in my mind. I felt that the only way for me to try to achieve personal and intellectual wholeness would be to attend a graduate school that could take my inquiry seriously and could also help nurture my faith in God. This search would occur at Harvard Divinity School and the Divinity School at the University of Chicago, where Dr. Benjamin Mays had completed his doctoral studies.

My first week at Harvard I constantly pinched myself to ensure that I was awake. For many years, I had dreamed of studying at this intellectual citadel. The best part about Harvard was its bookstores and cafes. At one point I laughed, noting that there were as many bookstores per block as storefront churches and liquor stores on a typical block in Chicago. I avidly collected books and spent many late evenings expanding my intellectual horizons.

Although enrolled at the Divinity School, which few elsewhere in the university knew about, I availed myself of resources throughout the school. I audited a business ethics course at the business school and saw firsthand Harvard's famous case-study method. I studied the history of American medicine at the college. My favorite intellectual pastime was walking over to listen to Alan Dershowitz's lectures on constitutional law. Dershowitz has become one of America's superstar lawyers, having represented such high-profile clients as Claus von Bulow and O. J. Simpson. In class he was brilliant, mixing case law with humorous anecdotes from the daily news into a Socratic-style argument. I especially appreciated the way he challenged the auditorium of future power lawyers to understand how the law works as a tool to protect the ruling class. He goaded students by prefacing his questions to them with comments like, "Now, Mr. Strauss, in four years you'll be a famous Wall Street lawyer, and the only poor people you'll come into contact with will be your maid and butler. Can you tell us what the Founding Fathers had in mind when they framed the Fourth Amendment? And why your maid and butler love the amendment, and you and your friends hate it?"

On some Sundays, instead of taking the subway to Roxbury, Boston's black community, I would go to the university's Memorial Church to hear Dr. Peter Gomes preach. From the elevated, white, wooden pulpit, he relished taking on traditional interpretations of biblical texts. He was one of the many fascinating, eccentric personalities that peppered the Harvard faculty. After the service, all of the students gathered at the chaplain's house for tea and conversation. I still marvel at how one gets perfect New England diction and accent inside the mouth of a short, black, Baptist preacher with a winning smile. Even more impressive to me was the manner in which Gomes made religion at Harvard come alive, drawing large numbers of students and faculty to the church. Years later, Gomes came to national attention for having authored a provocative work on the Bible, *The Good Book*, and for revealing that he is gay.

The Divinity School was a lively place that lacked a center. In a place with diverse theological orientations, building community was a constant challenge. Although it was a seminary, one could not assume any shared theological ground. Communication was painstaking, slow, measured. In retrospect, the need to communicate faith claims in such a diverse marketplace of theological starting points provided exceedingly important training for speaking theologically in the larger world. Students who spend their entire lives within the Christian theological circle, or any other circle, need to remember that God created many different villages, and loves the people of those villages as well. Responsible ministry in our pluralistic context must respect difference and otherness as gifts that enrich our own particularlity.

> Students who spend their lives within the Christian theological circle, or any other circle, need to remember that God created many different villages, and loves the people of those villages as well.

My favorite professor at Harvard was Father George MacRae, who taught the Introduction to the New Testament. He was a large, round, soft-spoken man and wore turtleneck shirts under his blazer. I found his voice spellbinding. I was such a devotee that I taped all of his lectures and listened to them at night. One day early in the semester, he opened his lecture on the biblical Acts of the Apostles by noting that it was a piece of literature similar to a modern novel and could not be regarded as reliable history. If he said anything after those words, I didn't hear it. My brain was wounded.

When class recessed, I hurried to my dorm room in Rockefeller Hall, got on my knees, and began to pray and to grieve. My spiritual foundations had been shaken by a man whom I regarded as a profound religious voice in the community. I discovered that other students had experienced a similar crisis of authority. When we asked Professor MacRae to help us work through the authority issues, he generously agreed to convene a special session for those who wished to discuss the personal implications of studying the Bible critically. MacRae listened patiently and responded that we were at a point at which we had to choose to become Christians. Our inheritance of belief nurtured by family and Sunday school had prepared us for this moment. Lacking an infallible text fallen from the sky, we could take the leap of faith, trusting in the God of the Bible, or we could be intellectually dishonest and claim that the Bible was something other than what it claims to be: a compilation of writings authored by fallible men and women moved by the Holy Spirit to record their journeys of faith. This explanation didn't help much at the time, but it gave us the hope and courage to carry on and to keep open minds. It also challenged us to become more serious about our personal faith.

Black students at the Divinity School gathered on Sunday evenings for worship, where we could allow the Spirit to move freely. Some of the best preaching I've ever heard happened when this beleaguered band of students struggled to keep the faith amid the onslaughts of a skeptical, liberal institution. Today, many of these former classmates have become the nation's premier preachers, theologians, and prophetic activists. I think of Frank Madison Reid (Baltimore); Fred Lucas (Brooklyn); Jesse Boyd (Denver); Kathy Gatson, Samuel Hogan, Eugene Rivers, and Ed McBride (Boston); Allan Callahan (Cambridge, Massachusetts); Melvin Brown, Eleanor Ivory, and Cheryl Sanders (Washington); Andy Cleo Lewter and Dexter Wise (Columbus, Ohio); Rita Dixon (Louisville); Marion Humphrey (Little Rock); Rodney Hunter (Newport News, Virginia); Thomas Scott (Atlanta); Isaac Canales (Los Angeles); Ralph Henley (Memphis); and Kenneth Hill (Nashville).

After visiting numerous churches in the Boston area, I realized that my spiritual, cultural, and intellectual needs were not being satisfied. A year and a half into seminary, a friend, Samuel Hogan, and I founded a small congregation in his apartment. We began with a weekly Bible study that included two single mothers, Marjory Brown and Betsy Stewart, and their very bright and energetic children, Lisa and Paul.

At the same time, Sam and I conducted a daily Bible teaching program on the radio. This was great fun and taught me a lot about presenting theology in a pluralistic, public context. Radio time was expensive, and after a year we were deep in debt. In our final week on the air we invited listeners to a reception at a community center in the South End. To our surprise, nearly a hundred people showed up. One distinguished white gentleman sized me up, then a slender seminarian, and said, "With such a big voice, I had imagined a much larger man." He should see me now. I have since grown into the voice.

After announcing that we were conducting a weekly Bible study, we increased the number of our friends to thirty. It was then that I approached Dean Krister Stendahl about permitting us to worship in the Divinity School chapel on Sundays. He was a creative spirit and agreed that it would be an interesting experiment. So there we were, a Spirit-filled congregation singing, praising, and preaching amid the ivy of Harvard. One day the eminent professor John Kenneth Galbraith was walking his dog in front of the chapel and paused to inquire about the source of tambourine noise in his affluent neighborhood. When I left a year later the Good Shepherd Church had grown into a congregation of more than one hundred people, and continues to thrive under the Reverend Hogan's leadership.

Although Harvard was challenging, the University of Chicago was strenuous in the extreme. Since reading Dr. Mays's autobiography, *Born to Rebel*, I had determined to pursue a Ph.D. there. But I always recalled his chilling observation about those who began but never completed the degree at Chicago.

Regardless of one's previous academic record, he takes a risk when he announces his intention to earn a Ph.D., especially at an institution like the University of Chicago. It was the prevailing opinion that the university made it difficult for those who sought the degree, and it was rumored that approximately half of those who started out in the department in which I was enrolled failed to accomplish their goal. I knew a few persons who had failed their Ph.D. work at the University of Chicago, and it seemed to me that they were never quite the same thereafter. A man who seeks a doctorate and fails to earn it seems to go through life either apologizing for his shortcoming or overcompensating for the failure.[1]

Despite having wonderfully supportive professors like Don Browning, Robin Lovin, Franklin Gamwell, and Chicago Theological Seminary President C. Shelby Rooks, Chicago was an austere, demanding, cerebral community where I felt like a lonesome traveler.

During those difficult years of isolation, despair, and self-doubt I made missteps that disappointed and hurt my family and friends. But in the midst of personal failure, crisis, and lack of faith, I was sustained by the God who offers grace and mercy to lost sheep everywhere. I had often quoted the verse, "If you confess your faults, God is faithful and just and will forgive your sins and heal you of all unrighteousness" (1 John 1:9). Today my hope, joy, and determination to journey onward, no matter what comes, are grounded on that verse.

In 1984 I returned to Cambridge to join Dean George Rupp's administration at Harvard Divinity School. I had the good fortune of working alongside a phenomenal teacher and administrator, Sister Mary Hennessey. Many of my former teachers became colleagues who pushed me to complete my dissertation. I am grateful to Preston Williams, Harvey Cox, and Constance Buchanan for their encouragement. Despite a challenging job at an exciting institution, I was restless and unhappy. Amid my period of despair and wandering, I met the extraordinary woman who would become my travel partner in life. On February 11, 1984, Harvard's black graduate students hosted a Black History Month reception in the lobby of the Kennedy School of Government for students, staff, and faculty in the Harvard community. My eye fell on a lovely and energetic personality across the lobby who seemed to be standing in the middle of traffic and directing it. Cheryl was a graduating senior at Harvard Medical School and on her way back to Houston to begin her residency.

After four months of dating, as we prayed about and discussed our future, we decided that marriage should be part of our journey. Following her departure for Houston, and my acceptance of a teaching position at the Colgate-Rochester Divinity School, we carried on a long-distance engagement until we were wed in June 1986, whereupon she moved to Rochester, New York, to complete her medical training. In Rochester, where the snow falls in May and the sky blushes in a hundred shades of gray, I was able to complete my dissertation under the stern and loving encouragement of Larry Greenfield, Toinette Eugene, and James Evans.

On a frigid Chicago day in February 1985, I received my Ph.D. It was 13 degrees below zero that Friday the thirteenth, but I felt warm and blessed to have completed this part of my educational journey. As President Hanna Gray handed over the diploma, I smiled and thought about Dr. Benjamin Mays and all who had helped me to avoid the failure of which he had written. Since that time, I have had the honor of serving on the faculties of Colgate Rochester Divinity School and the Candler School of Theology at Emory University. But after nine years of teaching I grew restless, concerned that my gifts were not being effectively used to affect the lives of urban residents. I was fortunate to have an opportunity to join the staff of the Ford Foundation in New York City. In chapter 5, I will have more to say about my experience as a minister in the nation's largest and most prestigious secular foundation, and will offer suggestions to clergy and church workers about how to approach foundations in search of support for faith-based community service programs. My experience at the foundation has provided insight into the kind of religious leadership most likely to command the respect, collaboration, and possibly financial support of the vast nonprofit and philanthropic communities.

Learning What Works

I now have the honor of providing leadership for the nation's largest historically black seminary, the Interdenominational Theological Center in Atlanta. At ITC we strive to be a resource for community problem solving by preparing religious leaders who are intellectually keen, politically sophisticated, economically savvy, culturally sensitive, family friendly, technologically literate, and, above all, spiritually astute. In chapter 6, I will discuss further the profile of the new clergy that our nation needs and awaits.

I have opened this book by describing some of the experiences that have unfolded in my relatively young life and that contribute to my outlook on life and ministry. I will allude to other portions of my life journey at relevant points in the chapters that follow. By lifting up some of the salient moments of my life, I hope to remind readers that there are young black males from working-class, inner-city families and Pentecostal churches who stand ready to contribute to the betterment of the church and the larger society. In one sense, my story also underscores that certain experiences work constructively to direct the boundless energies of youth.

> There is a role for every citizen, every believer, every church, every nonprofit agency, and every government organization to play in reknitting the unraveled fabric of civil society in our cities.

Church involvement, part-time employment, rewards for intellectual performance, protection from negative influences in the community, and travel beyond one's village all work. We need more, not less, of these opportunities. There is a role for every citizen, every believer, every church, every nonprofit agency, and every government organization to play in reknitting the unraveled fabric of civil society in our cities. As the refrain in the muffler commercial advises, "We can pay now or we can pay later." Whatever we do as citizens, church people, or public agencies, we should do it with dispatch, recalling the words of Dr. Benjamin Mays's wonderful poem, "God's Minute":

> I have only one minute
> only sixty seconds in it
> forced upon me, can't refuse it
> didn't seek it, didn't choose it;
> It's up to me to use it,
> I will suffer if I lose it, must give account
> if I abuse it,
> just a tiny minute, but . . .
> eternity is in it.

2 SAFE HAVENS

A s I write, houses of worship are being burned in America. According to the U.S. Justice Department, approximately 180 black churches were victimized by arson between January 1995 and June 1996, and the ugly trend continues. This fact adds painful irony to the black church's historical status as the *safest* place on earth. During the rash of burnings in the mid-1990s, a reporter asked me, "Why are they burning black churches as opposed to civil rights organization offices?" I responded that, in the case of racially motivated burnings, the perpetrators were attempting to strike at the soul of black folk, to paraphrase W. E. B. Du Bois. By assaulting these communities of faith, they disrespect the oldest and most beloved institution in the black community. The attacks are designed to hurt deeply and to deflate hope as much as they aim to counter

29

the justice-seeking vitalities of the church. The churches have been the one place where people of low status felt important and where all the names of the children were known. Those who trample these sacred trusts are, in effect, spitting on our grandmothers' graves.

The Ecology of the Black Church

Let me offer a "worm's eye view" of what I am calling the core culture of the black church. In so doing I hope to orient readers to the distinctive ecology of faith communities that nurtures hope and empowers people to engage in public activism. In a sense, this chapter offers a portrait of the black church as it has been. The next chapter will report on how the church is evolving in view of the societal changes set in motion during the civil rights movement.

A Multisensory Worship Experience

One of the significant and fascinating legacies of slavery is the manner in which African Americans organized the precious hours when they were not working. Given the difficulty and dehumanizing nature of their work, they created sacred space as a zone of ultimate freedom. In worship, the mind, emotions, and other sensory capacities were engaged in transcending the banality of evil. Aware that they would soon have to return to the boredom and dread of field work, slaves threw themselves fully into the worship experience.

This legacy has shaped contemporary black worship wherein all of the senses are acknowledged, engaged, and blessed. All worship is in some sense a sacred drama, a dance with the gods. In black church worship, the drama is driven by the beat of the drums and the motion of call-and-response preaching. Choir robes and clergy vestments provide splashes of color. Brass horns and tambourines, guitars and synthesizers electrify the air, permeated by the aromas of an elaborate Sunday feast wafting from the church kitchen next door. In this space, there is lots of touching, hugging, holy kissing—reaching out. Amid this drama, one finds satisfaction at the core, knowing that within this crowd of loving, caring people one is in the safest place in the world. For people who have been oppressed, worship has always been valued for its capacity to provide a window into the reign and commonwealth of God. As the scripture says, "When the righteous cry for help, the Lord hears, and rescues them from all their troubles" (Psalm 34:17). Much of that deliverance occurs in worship.

The internal logic or ecology of worship seeks to facilitate a palpable sense of God's existence and love. Theologically, black worship coheres around the image of a powerful and sovereign God, but one who permits humans to become partners in overcoming the damage to creation caused by the many forms of sin. As Brooklyn pastor Dr. Johnny Ray Youngblood puts it, "God acts in history with one arm tied behind his back." Hence, worship must empower finite and frail people if God's purposes are to be accomplished.

> *For people who have been oppressed, worship has always been valued for its capacity to provide a window into the reign and commonwealth of God.*

For black churches, access to God is provided through the Holy Spirit. The spirit realm is conceived as one of freedom. Slaves who were shackled could experience a bit of absolute freedom by abandoning themselves to God's spirit. Through the careful coordination of visual, audio, olfactory, and tactile stimuli, good worship becomes a form of spiritual therapy in which human wholeness is actualized through communion with God. God is felt and known through worship that engages the senses. Authentic worship is, in Paul Tillich's terms, a "theonomous" encounter in which participants may relate to a God who abhors dichotomies and who reconciles the rational and emotional dimensions of human being, the sacred and the secular, right brain and left, the yin and the yang.

Although most African American worship reflects an appreciation for multiple sensory stimulation, congregations that have a Protestant, evangelical heritage in large part have not integrated liturgical practices such as the use of incense, bells, silence, and elaborate eucharistic rituals (Holy Communion). These practices, generally more common in the Anglican and Roman Catholic traditions, direct praise toward God and stimulate the senses through different means. Authentically wholistic liturgy should integrate and even experiment with the many ways of encountering the holy.

Intimate Communal Prayer

In the absence of a formal ritual of confession, the pastoral prayer offered for parishioners who approach the altar is an empowering moment. As the congregants stand before God and the pastor, they are invited toward consciousness of their individual shortcomings. This is a time for them to enter what Martin Buber called an "I–Thou" relationship with the deity. But it is also an opportunity for community building. A skillful prayer leader who understands commonalities in the human condition can weave detached individuals into a larger community that stands together in need of grace. In this way, communal prayer challenges the privatizing tendencies that are always present in the faith journey.

In addition to the space and time for intimate communion with God, each congregant receives emotional license to sense God providing the needed form of therapy and empowerment. Persons who may never visit a professional counselor or therapist are encouraged to do grief work and careful introspection, to experience vulnerability, and to make resolutions to reform their behavior in the future.

Cathartic Expressivism

Often when the senses and the human spirit are engaged in a powerful way, people feel compelled to express through emotion and action what may be ineffable. *Shouting* refers to a wide range of behaviors—from the joyful ecstasy of praise to the heart-rending anguish of unconsoled grief—that express the worshipers' immediate sense of God's presence. During designated moments of formal worship, shouters may stand, clap their hands, walk about, dance, leap, weep, speak in tongues, kneel, hug someone, or lay prostrate on the floor in response to an overwhelming encounter with what

Rudolph Otto referred to as the *mysterium tremendum,* or the awe-inspiring holiness of God. This liturgical accommodation to the worshipers' need and desire to encounter the holy in this personal, embodied manner encourages the release of powerful energies which might otherwise be suppressed to the detriment of the person.

Another means of expressing internal concerns in a public forum is the ritual of *testifying.* In some traditions, testimonies constitute art forms that conform to a formula including at least five basic elements: (1) an opening comment expressing respect to God and the community elders; (2) a declaration of one's current upright spiritual condition; (3) an account of the trials, temptations, and tribulations endured in the past; (4) words of gratitude for one's current victorious state; and (5) a solicitation of the prayers and support of the congregation.

One of the interesting features of "shouting" black churches, since all of them are not, is the presence of uniformed nurses stationed strategically near the altar or around the sanctuary to supervise the cathartic ritual process. Nurses may simply stand near the ecstatic worshiper to fan them and protect them from injury, or may remove the worshiper from the service to provide quiet space and support. The nurse ensures that the process unfolds safely. When problems occur, the nurse intervenes to stop inappropriate or nonspiritual occurrences. Along with the pastor, the nurse supervises the delicate process of what anthropologist Victor Turner refers to as the "reincorporation" of the ecstatic, "liminal" agent back into the life of the community. Ultimately, the pastor seeks to insure that the ecstatic moment will be translated into ongoing personal moral renewal.

Most black pastors try to facilitate a dynamic, dialectical relationship between the dominant poles of the moral life articulated by William James, between ascetic striving for justice and moral perfection, and the mystical, playful disengagement from the stress of moral life. The best of the black church tradition focuses steadily on both personal and social transformation. It emphasizes that personal conversion, moral renewal, and sanctification should manifest themselves in acts of justice, charity, and service in the wider world. Martin Luther King experienced this firsthand, and also sought to encourage and monitor this process in church members who followed him from the sanctuary to the streets.

Triumphant Singing

I grew up in a church with an impressive music ministry, including several choirs that wore magnificent robes and moved in carefully choreographed ways to the beat of drums. I often played the drums as a youth. We believed that the Hammond organ, drums, and guitars could help people move to the rhythms and facilitate an experience of the holy. We thought of God as one who enjoyed rhythm, for God had created the rhythms of the heartbeat, the ebb and flow of ocean waves, and the changing of nature's seasons. Thus the drums had an integrating function. When they were played properly, we expected the Spirit to move and to transform the mundane worship space into a holy site.

The black church tradition emphasizes that personal conviction, moral renewal, and sanctification should manifest themselves in acts of justice, charity, and service in the wider world.

In such worship cultures, the songs of the choir are carefully selected and orchestrated to inspire hope and triumphant faith among people who are acquainted with the pain of oppression. Songs such as "I'm a Soldier in the Army of the Lord" or "Victory Shall Be Mine" can empower people to become fearless moral agents who struggle hopefully for a good community and a just society.

It should be noted, however, that not all of the music in the black church is "marching" music, or upbeat and quick-paced. I am fascinated by the manner in which the organ and the soft chanting of the choir can calm an ecstatically charged worship atmosphere. Chants mediate the return from a mystical mountaintop experience to the mundane reality of everyday life.

With regard to the therapeutic and preparatory function of black sacred music, Molefi Asante has observed that

Singing sets the stage or mood by preparing the audience emotionally and physically for the preacher, whose communication
task is made easier because of the audience receptivity. Singing,
. . . although instructive, is much more palliative; it soothes the
emotions and draws the congregation together. . . . the preacher
inherits an attentive audience by virtue of the choir's work.[1]

Skillful prayer leaders help bind disparate individuals in a
praying, striving community. Skillful worship leaders guide ecstatic
worshipers into an ongoing process of faith development and
social responsibility. Similarly, skillful music ministers or musicians assist worshipers in focusing attention on the agenda in worship, whether rejoicing, giving, or listening to the sermon. The
work of good worship is the responsibility of many people.

Congregational singing and song development can be a spon-
taneous and democratic process. People who have song ideas or
inspirations can ask the musicians and choir for assistance in shaping the song so that all can sing. This practice seems to be a carry-
over from slave culture, in which songs were generated sponta-
neously during work and play, and also from some West African
religious cultures, where one can observe a similar creative process.
During my visits to villages in Senegal and Ghana, the singers
would incorporate my visit into a refrain.

Politically Empowering Religious Education

Although most black denominations have owned and operated their
own publishing houses for decades, the theological and cultural content of the material generally did not differ greatly from the material
produced by their white counterparts. Since the time of the civil
rights and black power movements, many black churches have
sought to revise their educational ministries to be more relevant to
the cultural and political needs of a new generation. Many churches
have abandoned the literature and agenda developed by white evangelical Christian educators in favor of materials that facilitate the nurture of both Christian and black identity. Black religious educators
are currently publishing a growing variety of culturally appropriate

materials and convening regular meetings to expand this agenda. Perhaps the largest annual gathering of black Christian educators is sponsored by the Hampton University Ministers Conference.

In Chicago, Dr. Jeremiah A. Wright, Jr., of the Trinity United Church of Christ is explicit in his desire to design a church culture that is "unashamedly Christian and unapologetically black." Toward that end, he requires all clergy and members to become active in Bible classes. He teaches the clergy group and assigns texts from black theologians who advance a liberation agenda. Wright's sermons set the tone and angle of political analysis pursued in all of the Bible classes. In addition, he has been assisted in developing a culturally appropriate curriculum by Dr. Jawanza Kunjufu, a well-known Afrocentric eduational consultant.

One of Dr. Kunjufu's critiques of public education can help evaluate the educational component of a local congregation's ministry. He suggests a need for "coaches" rather than instructors in order to increase levels of student retention and achievement, especially among black boys. He suggests that "Instructors specialize in dispensing information," he writes. "Coaches have the ability to combine subject matter and learning styles with identity and self-esteem."[2] In black churches, the most effective teachers are coaches whose involvement in a child's character development may exceed that of the parents. Single-parent families have greatly appreciated this type of support for youth development.

> *In black churches, the most effective teachers are coaches whose involvement in a child's character development may exceed that of the parents.*

Prophetic, Imaginative Preaching

Within the context of worship an event that deeply engages the senses, preaching is the central sacred moment. Seeking to define the sacred, the famous historian of religion Mircea Eliade has noted that "for people in traditional societies religion is a means of extending the world spatially upward so that communication with the other world becomes ritually possible, and extending it temporally backward so that the paradigmatic acts of the gods and mythical ancestors can be continually re-enacted and indefinitely recoverable."[3]

This comment illumines the genius of black preaching. Each week the preacher is expected to undertake the priestly task of mediating an encounter with the holy through the spatial and temporal extension of reality. While most interpreters of black preaching understand the preacher as a prophet and a moral teacher, I am calling attention to a subtle dimension of rhetorical leadership that has been inadequately examined.

Consider the following illustration of the transformative power of imaginative sacred language from Zora Neale Hurston's novel, *Jonah's Gourd Vine*. I quote the text at length in order to convey the beauty and poetic cadence of traditional folk preaching. Proclaiming the manner of Christ's redemptive journey to earth, the preacher declares:

I see Jesus
Leaving heben with all of His grandeur
Disrobing Hisself of His matchless honor,
Yielding up de scepter of revolvin' worlds
Clothing himself in de garment of humanity
Coming into de world to rescue his friends.
Two thousand years have went by on their rusty ankles
But with the eye of faith, I can see Him.
Look down from His high towers of elevation
I can hear Him when He walks about the golden streets
I can hear 'em ring under His footsteps . . .
I can see Him step out upon the rim bones of nothing
Crying I am de way
De truth and de light . . .
I see Him grab de throttle
Of de well ordered train of mercy
I see kingdoms crush and crumble
Whilst the archangels held de winds in the corner chambers
I see Him arrive on dis earth
And walk de streets thirty and three years. . . .
I see Him walking beside de sea of Galilee wid His disciples

This declaration gendered on His lips
"Let us go on to the other side."
God A'mighty! . . .
I can see him with de eye of faith.
When He went from Pilate's house
With the crown of seventy-two wounds upon His head
I can see Him as He mounted Calvary and hung upon de cross
    for our sins. . . .
De mountains fell to their rocky knees when He cried
"My God, my God! Why hast thou forsaken me?"
The mountains fell to their rocky knees and trembled like a beast
From the stroke of the master's axe
One angel took the flinches of God's eternal power
And bled the veins of the earth
One angel that stood at the gate with a flaming sword
Was so well pleased with his power
Until he pierced the moon with his sword
And she ran down in blood
And de sun,
Batted her fiery eyes and put on her judgment robe
And laid down in the cradle of eternity
And rocked herself into sleep and slumber
He died until the great belt in the wheel of time
And de geological strata fell aloose
And a thousand angels rushed to de canopy of heben
With flamin' swords in their hands
And placed their feet upon blue ether's bosom, and
    looked back at the dazzling throne
And de arc angels had veiled their faces
And de throne was draped in mournin'
And de orchestra had struck silence for the space of half an hour
Angels had lifted their harps to de weepin' willows
And God had looked off to-wards immensity
And blazin' worlds fell off His teeth
And about that time Jesus groaned on de cross, and
Dropped His head in the locks of His shoulder and said,
    "It is finished, it is finished."
And then de chambers of hell exploded
And de damnable spirits
Come up from de Sodomistic world and rushed into de smoky
    camps of eternal night,

And cried, "Woe! Woe! Woe!"
And then de Centurion cried out,
"Surely this is the Son of God."
And about dat time,
De angel of Justice unsheathed his flamin' sword and ripped
     de veil of the temple
And de High Priest vacated his office
And then de sacrificial energy penetrated de mighty strata
And quickened de bones of de prophets
And they arose from their graves and walked about in de streets
     of Jerusalem
I heard de whistle of de damnation train
That pulled out from Garden of Eden loaded wid cargo goin'
     to hell
Ran at break-neck speed all de way through de law
All de way through de prophetic age
All de way through de reign of kings and judges—
Plowed her way thru de Jurdan
And on her way to Calvary, when she blew for de switch
Jesus stood out on her track like a rough-backed mountain
And she threw her cow-catcher in His side and His blood
     ditched de train
He died for our sins.
Wounded in the house of His friends.
That's where I got off de damnation train
And dat's where you must get off, ha!
For in that mor-ornin', ha!
When we shall all be delegates, ha!
To dat Judgment Convention
When de two trains of Time shall meet on de trestle
And wreck de burning axles of de unformed ether
And de mountains shall skip like lambs
When Jesus shall place one foot on de neck of de sea, ha!
One foot on de dry land
When His chariot wheels shall be running hub-deep in fire
He shall take His friends thru the open bosom of an
     un-clouded sky,
And place in their hands de "hosanna" fan
And they shall stand 'round and 'round his beatific throne
And praise His name forever, Amen.[4]

Words can create worlds. The black preacher, through the virtuosity of imaginative, narrative, lyrical, and poetic language, and the co-creativity of a responsive congregation, brings the sacred and human realms together. The preacher calls down the Spirit and calls the masses up to the mountaintop where the two may meet. Since preaching in antiphony invites the participation of the listener, one experiences the word of God in the midst of a dialogue; God may be perceived as a trustworthy conversation partner. Hence the proclaimed word does not belong to the congregation's elite class, usually male, middle-aged clergy, but to all who have ears to hear and mouths to talk back.

English professor Hortense Spillers has observed that the black preacher "weaves analogy and allegory into the sermon, comparing and juxtaposing contemporary problems in morality with and alongside ancient problems in morality."[5] Black preachers may be responsible for keeping alive the great tradition of storytelling in American culture. They provide a narrative framework within which hearers can interpret public life in a compelling way. The narrative draws people in, inviting them to evaluate the moral hygiene of the state, market, and civil society. They use biblical categories and themes such as exodus, crucifixion, resurrection, sin, and redemption to help people think historically and critically about the condition of the community.

The black preacher, through the virtuosity of imaginative, lyrical, and poetic language, and the co-creativity of a responsive congregation, brings the sacred and human realms together.

For instance, preachers have employed the exodus motif, the most famous in black sermonic discourse, to portray the African American struggle for justice as continuous with, and parallel to, ancient Israel's struggle to escape from Egypt. Portraying the black experience through this biblical lens offered a bold and prophetic challenge to the primary assumption of American civil religion, namely that America was the new Israel sent on an "errand into the wilderness" to establish a free, God-fearing nation. Black preachers transgressed the dominant narrative, characterizing America as the new Egypt guilty of oppressing a new generation of slaves.

Throughout his ministry, Dr. King weaved the black story with the biblical story to rally followers to keep the faith during difficult times. Note how he inspired bus boycotters in Montgomery, Alabama:

> We are here this evening because we are tired now, but let us say that we are not here advocating violence. We have overcome that. I want it to be known throughout Montgomery and throughout this nation that we are a Christian people. We believe in the Christian religion. We believe in the teachings of Jesus. The only weapon that we have in our hands this evening is the weapon of protest. . . . This is the glory of America, with all of its faults. . . . The great glory of American democracy is the right to protest for right.[6]

The Spiritualities of the Black Church

In addition to describing these major features of black church culture, it might be useful to identify some of the major styles of thought about spirituality on today's landscape.[7] The current hunger for spirituality throughout society assumes many forms— Eastern meditation, dietary asceticism, Pentecostalism, and so on. In the African American community I have observed at least seven traditions of seeking spiritual communion. These traditions have important implications for the future shape of congregational life in the African American community, the leadership needs of those congregations, and the theological training of the leaders.

1. The *evangelical* tradition seeks a deeper knowledge of God's word, following conversion, through study, teaching, and preaching. This tradition is represented by Dr. William Bentley, who founded the National Black Evangelical Association (Chicago).

2. The *holiness* tradition seeks purity of life and thought through the disciplines of fasting, renunciation, and prayer. This pattern has been powerfully embodied by many spiritual leaders; it is difficult to identify a person widely known. However, I would

like to suggest Dr. Arenia C. Mallory, who was the principal of the Saints Junior Academy in Lexington, Mississippi, a school operated by the Church of God in Christ to prepare future leaders of the denomination.

3. The *charismatic* tradition seeks empowerment through the Holy Spirit by tarrying, in the search for spiritual gifts, and in prayer. William J. Seymour, the modern father of black Pentecostalism, represents this tradition.

4. The *social justice* tradition seeks public righteousness through community activism, political advocacy, and preaching. This spiritual tradition is compellingly represented by Rev. Vernon Johns, the pastor who preceded Dr. King at the Dexter Avenue Baptist Church in Montgomery.

5. The *Afrocentric* tradition seeks to celebrate the halcyon days of the African past and to affirm black identity in the present through cultural displays and identification with African history and rituals. This tradition is represented by Rev. George Alexander McGuire, who founded the African Orthodox Church as part of the Garvey movement.

6. The *contemplative* tradition of spirituality seeks intimacy with God and employs the disciplines of prayer and meditation. In the black church tradition, the theologian and mystic Howard Thurman has been viewed as a towering symbol of this style of spiritual existence.

7. The *new age* nontheistic tradition seeks peace of mind and harmony with nature through meditation, chanting, and music. This is a relatively new and numerically small expression in the black community; however, I would suggest that the popular singer Dionne Warwicke exemplifies new age spirituality by appearing on television to market counseling from psychics and from people who claim to be able to foretell events.

The liturgical and spiritual dimensions of black church culture that I have discussed are not exhaustive. I regard them as the constitutive ritual practices found in the vast majority of black churches. This ensemble of internal liturgical practices nurtures the

Spirituality Traditions	Spiritual End (*telos*)	Spiritual Disciplines	Spiritual Exemplar
Evangelical	Knowledge of God's Word	Teaching, preaching, study	William Bentley
Holiness	Purity of life and thought	Fasting, prayer, renunciation	Arenia C. Mallory
Charismatic	Empowerment through the Spirit	Tarrying, seeking spiritual gifts	William J. Seymour
Social Justice	Public righteousness	Community activism, political activity	Vernon Johns
Afrocentric	Celebration of black identity	Cultural displays of African heritage	George Alexander McGuire
Contemplative	Intimacy with God	Prayer, meditation	Howard Thurman
New Age	Peace of mind	Meditation, chanting, music	Dionne Warwicke

Traditions of African American Spirituality

parishioners' sense of responsibility for the world outside, and their capacity to do something about social evil.

The Social Witness of the Black Church

This rich culture has also coexisted with a variety of responses to the social crisis. Many onlookers have wondered why black churches are often very involved in secular political affairs, and why many clergy run for elective office. I have some ideas. These ministers all seek to apply theology in the public arena but do so in different ways. It might be helpful to keep in mind that these clergy have different goals, strategies, and theological justifications for their political ministries.

Pragmatic Accommodationism

Since Reconstruction, the vast majority of black churches have adopted *pragmatic accommodationism* in seeking social empowerment. The leaders of the largest black denominations, such as the National Baptist Convention, the Church of God in Christ, and the African Methodist Episcopal Church, are generally expected by their members to operate from this perspective, avoiding extremely conservative or liberal political views.

The moral end these churches seek is a peaceful, predictable *social order* in which they may acquire and enjoy what is thought to be a fair distribution of goods such as education, housing, health care, and jobs. The primary strategy employed to achieve social order is *cooperation* and *compromise* with the political and corporate status quo. In order to make progress, a pragmatic clergyperson must play the political game as effectively as her or his opponents insisting that the rules for distributing goods be neutral and applied fairly to all players. Making deals is not simply acceptable but is morally required in order to produce for one's constituents the most favorable balance of good over bad consequences.

> *In order to make progress, a pragmatic clergyperson must play the political game as effectively as her or his opponents, insisting that the rules for distributing goods be neutral and applied fairly to all players.*

The most frequently used warrant or metaphor of justification is the portrayal of God as *Creator*. The pragmatists believe that God has provided a bountiful earth with resources adequate for every living creature. Scarcity is not the problem; rather, human will and faulty distributive schemes are responsible for poverty and inequality. God desires that God's children have all of the basic goods necessary for personal development. This belief empowers accommodationist clergy to cooperate with the system in order to wrest the maximum amount of welfare provisions for their less fortunate parishioners. They do not seek to change the basic structures of representative democratic government or market capitalism. Rather they seek reforms in the political economy that would

accrue to the benefit of excluded, less-advantaged groups. Accommodationist churches and clergy tend to embrace middle-class values
and aspirations, and are invested in expanding the American dream
of prosperity.

Prophetic Radicalism

I characterize the second group of politically active clergy as *prophetic radicals*. This strategy stretches back to slave preachers of the eigh-
teenth and nineteenth centuries such as Gabriel Prosser, David
Walker, and Nat Turner. Although Martin Luther King articulated
this approach to political activism most fully, it was embodied most
compellingly in Adam Clayton Powell, the first African American
clergyperson in the twentieth century to serve in Congress. Since the
civil rights movement the strategy has been embraced by Rev. Jesse
Jackson, although he is a complicated figure who blends features of
the first two political ministry styles. Large numbers of clergy from
many denominations subscribe to this option, especially clergy
from the Progressive National Baptist Convention, which separated
from the National Baptist Convention in part over differences in
political theology. One can find significant pockets of the prophetic
orientation in all of the denominations of the Congress of National
Black Churches, established by Bishop John Hurst Adams of the
African Methodist Episcopal Church. The growing popularity of this
perspective is due in part to the growing number of black clergy pursuing formal theological education in places where they are likely to
encounter the writings of black liberation theologians such as James
Cone (Union Theological Seminary), Jacquelyn Grant (ITC), and
Cain Hope Felder (Howard University).

Prophetic radicals pursue uncompromisingly the end of *social
justice*. In the American context, this involves a radical restructuring
of the free-market capitalist economy. Their analysis of America's
social problems focuses on the root causes of economic inequality,
and seeks to limit the acquisition of private wealth. In the democratic socialist vision which they embrace, the state would prohibit
dramatic economic disparities and seek full employment.

The chief means for pursuing justice are *confrontation* and *negotiation*. Rather than cooperating with the political status quo in order to increase their share of the common "pie," prophetic radicals initiate dramatic actions such as marches and boycotts, aimed at evoking a crisis that will attract attention and build popular support for radical change. According to such clergypersons, reform is not adequate to correct the problems of poverty, unemployment, ignorance, racism, sexism, environmental abuse, and so on. Radical transformation of public institutions and of human spirits is warranted and essential. Part of the genius of Dr. King's leadership, former professor and sitting congresswoman Eleanor Holmes Norton has observed, was his capacity to brilliantly employ both confrontation and negotiation. Recall that in his last planned campaign he planned to return to Washington with thousands of poor people to shut down the federal government and to press claims for economic justice. That kind of bold, risky action stands in sharp contrast to the more conciliatory and pragmatic strategies of many of King's own disciples.

> *Prophetic radicals initiate dramatic actions such as marches and boycotts, aiming at evoking a crisis that will attract attention and build popular support for radical change.*

Radical clergy commonly depict God as *liberator* and *judge*. As the Hebrew prophets held political authorities to divine accountability, these clergy live in tension with the status quo and seek its radical transformation. Their responsibility is to call the nation to higher levels of moral reasoning, to advocate a move from enlightened self-interest to sacrificial action on behalf of the common good. This was part of the mission and achievement of Dr. King's "I Have a Dream" oration.

Redemptive Nationalism

I characterize the third community of leaders as *redemptive nationalists*. Since the beginning of the African presence in the New World, there have been black Christian nationalists such as Martin Delaney and Bishop Henry McNeal Turner of the African Methodist Episcopal Church. More recently this option has been articulated by Albert B. Cleage, Jr., founder of the Shrine of the Black Madonna in Detroit and Atlanta. The most vigorous advocates in this tradition are not Christian but Muslims, including Malcolm X and Louis Farrakhan.

Redemptive nationalists seek to establish a *separate black nation* in which the dignity and human rights of black people will be secure. In the 1920s, Marcus Garvey and his ecclesial counterpart, Rev. George Alexander McGuire, urged blacks to return to Africa. Following the collapse of Garvey's organization, the Universal Negro Improvement Association, Elijah Muhammad revised this goal. He argued that a separate tract of land in the United States or somewhere in the Caribbean should be made available for African Americans. We should note that the potency and attractiveness of black nationalist ideas are heightened in times when the socioeconomic status of blacks is threatened. Although few blacks embrace this social vision in its most radical form, large segments of the black community subscribe to a thin version of nationalist ideology. Even blacks who have fulfilled the American dream believe that blacks should control the core institutions within their geographic and cultural communities. This perspective seems to mirror the experience of white ethnic groups.

Black nationalist sentiments have spawned at least two interesting expressions in the twentieth century, one among black Catholics and the other among African American Jews. During the 1990s, Catholic priest George Stallings established the Imani Temple in Washington to make Catholicism more appealing to its disaffected members and to attract new ones. Stallings has sought to fuse the traditional Catholic mass with contemporary African American cultural expressions. Catholics who follow Stalling wear African clothing and vestments during worship, sing gospel music, and practice ecstatic praise behavior such as lifting hands and shouting "Amen" during the sermon. Increasingly, this pattern of worship is appearing in conventional Roman Catholic parishes in the black community. I will have more to say in the next chapter about the infusion of "Afrocentric aesthetics" into black worship.

Historically, there have been numerous communities of blacks who have identified with Judaism. These groups were largest in New York City prior to the Great Depression; many adherents were from the Caribbean. Note that the Rastafarians, a religio-cultural sect in Jamaica, incorporated numerous elements of Judaism into their belief system. Perhaps the best-known group of black Jews is the original African Hebrew Israelite community in Chicago. The organization has maintained a community in Dimona, Israel, for many years and has been the object of considerable scrutiny from the media and government.

Nationalists tend to cultivate an ambiguous relationship to the political and economic status quo, a relationship that may be described as *opportunistic*. That is, they engage the system in carefully calculated ways, such as through voting or by seeking elective office, in order to advance their particular interests while minimizing any future obligations or loyalties to secular civil authorities. They will play the political game, but only begrudgingly and, often, cynically. They would affirm the conservative commentator George F. Will's observation that "politics may be bad but it makes many good things possible."

These clergypersons tend to use the metaphor of God as *redeemer* of the lost and fragmented nations of the African diaspora. Similar to the prophetic radicals, they call the status quo to judgment and press it to actualize the ideals in the Constitution and Declaration of Independence. But they exhibit no special allegiance to the United States, and would prefer to have a separate land and government rather than to assimilate within or to transform the current system.

The political orientation of this community has evolved since the civil rights movement in ways roughly parallel to the emergence of conservative evangelicals or the religious right. In the 1950s and 1960s, Malcolm X and other nationalists eschewed political involvement, arguing that it was the devil's business and that they were not citizens of the American republic to begin with. But by the

1980s nationalists had become very savvy about political involvement and began to concentrate their efforts on electing their own
"homegrown" candidates. Although it
is exciting to see religious groups, previously on the margins of political life,
moving into the center and hopefully
reenergizing   our   anemic   electoral
processes, I am concerned that many of
these new political theologians do not
have a robust, inclusive vision of the
common good. For many of them, politics is an instrument with which to
impose their parochial vision of the
good community on everyone else. Whereas Jerry Falwell aims at
Christianizing American public life, Martin Luther King tried to
expand it to include America's rich religious pluralism.

> *Nationalists engage the system
> in carefully calculated ways,
> such as through voting or by seeking
> elective office, in order to advance
> their particular interests while
> minimizing any future obligations
> or loyalties to secular civil authorities.*

Grassroots Revivalism

This discussion brings us to another segment of the black religious
community which has enormous religious and cultural energy in
urban America. I refer to this group as *grassroots revivalists*. This tradition includes the thousands of clergypersons who do not have
formal theological education and who often have ministries in
storefront buildings or homes. Early in the twentieth century Rev.
William J. Seymour, often described as the "father" of black Pentecostalism, helped define this orientation. In fact, there were African
American women engaged in Pentecostal revivalist ministries prior
to Seymour's emergence in Los Angeles in 1906. Indeed, some of
those women helped to launch and sustain Seymour's famous
Azusa Street revival, where he conducted daily revival and healing
services. These meetings attracted curious seekers from around the
globe, and Seymour's multiracial following aroused suspicion and
resentment at the time.

Revivalists seek *personal salvation* for all people and tend to be
disengaged from the political order, or relate to it with contempt.

Such clergy are primarily interested in the moral hygiene of their members and tend not to advocate political visions or to endorse specific parties and candidates. They employ the metaphor of God as *savior* to authorize their ministries.

Sociologists of religion often characterize these groups as escapist, otherworldly cults. If one probes further, however, a more complex picture emerges. For instance, Bishop Charles H. Mason, founder of the Church of God in Christ, publicly proclaimed that God would judge America because of her mistreatment of poor people and urged young parishioners to declare conscientious objector status during World War I. His political theology earned the attention of the Federal Bureau of Investigation decades before Dr. King was harassed by FBI Director J.

> *Revivalists seek personal salvation for all people and tend to be disengaged from the political order, or relate to it with contempt.*

Edgar Hoover. Also, when Rev. Jesse Jackson ran for president during the 1980s, I witnessed the mobilization of grassroots clergy behind the candidacy of a fellow preacher.

If the revivalists' level of political involvement increases as they evolve toward a more mainline orientation, I predict that they will follow the path of the pragmatic accommodationists. One wonders whether they could be radicalized to embrace Dr. King's agenda of economic justice. I think that it would require someone with Dr. King's mass appeal to persuade conservative Christians that this agenda is congruent with the "politics of Jesus" and that they should not embrace uncritically the message of an assimilated cultural Christianity, which has compromised the prophetic witness of most mainline churches.

Positive-Thought Materialism

The final segment of the religious leadership can be described as positive-thought materialists. This is a relatively new school of black religious expression, so there are few significant historical examples. Depression-era leaders such as Father Divine and Daddy Grace initi-

Political-Theological Orientation	Moral Ends	Moral Means	Justification
Pragmatic accommodationists	Social order	Cooperation	(God as) Creator
Prophetic radicals	Social justice	Confrontation	Liberator
Redemptive nationalists	Separate nation	Opportunistic engagement	Redeemer
Grassroots revivalists	Personal salvation	Indifference	Savior
Positive-thought materialists	Individual prosperity	Opportunistic engagement	Provider

Five Forms of Political Ministry

ated many of the practices and the ideology that the more recent groups have adopted. The best-known contemporary example of this tradition is the New York-based radio preacher Reverend Ike.

Positive-thought materialists actively seek neither social order, social justice, a separate nation, nor personal salvation. Rather, they seek to maximize their own *health, wealth, and success*. In order to acquire these goods, rigorous personal disciplines are prescribed. Followers are provided with self-improvement literature, audio tapes, courses of instruction, and mantras to repeat throughout the day. Similar to the nationalists, materialists tend to cultivate a public posture of *opportunistic engagement* in which they seek to use the system to advance their narrow interests. Unlike the nationalists, they tend to focus entirely on individual empowerment and have few ideas about community economic revitalization.

Materialists often speak of God as the *provider* of all of the goods necessary for a comfortable life. When they speak of God's blessings they refer almost entirely to material goods. Because many of their teachings seem at odds with traditional Christianity, especially the theology of the cross, there is considerable tension between this community and the larger, more conventional black Christian tradition.

This taxonomy of black religious life is a rough sketch, to be sure. However, I hope that it establishes clearly that there is no longer a monolithic "black church" wherein all of the adherents believe and behave in a uniform manner. There is bubbling variety in this stew, and there is a vigorous debate within the community about the future.

> *Materialists tend to focus entirely on individual empowerment and have few ideas about community economic revitalization.*

Although I have not tried to do so, this typology could be applied to white religious leaders and communities with interesting results. It would not be difficult to categorize leaders such as Billy Graham (accommodationist), William Sloane Coffin (radical), Jerry Falwell (nationalist), Jimmy Swaggart (revivalist), and Robert Schuller (materialist). Comparative analysis would highlight how certain religious communities perceive and respond to secular realities such as power and money. Also, we might discover that a group's socioeconomic class might be as significant as racial identity in shaping positive or negative attitudes toward political activism. The practical impact of this effort would be the identification of theological common ground to mobilize ecumenical Christian and interfaith coalitions aimed at poverty alleviation, racial reconciliation, and religious tolerance.

I have tried in this chapter to provide a portrait of the black church as it has existed for many generations. Historically, it has been the safest place on earth for blacks because it has been the spiritual, emotional, cultural, political, educational, economic, and intellectual center of the community. But the revolutions of the 1960s evoked changes that are now becoming evident in black church culture. I report on some of the most prominent trends in the next chapter.

3 THE TEMPEST

The Black Church since the Civil Rights Movement

If you were to ask the average person what changes have occurred in the black church since the death of Martin Luther King, most either would have no idea or would think the question absurd. It's like the old joke, "How many deacons does it take to change a light bulb?" The punch line: "What do you mean, change?" Many people doubt that any changes have occurred in this most mature, bedrock institution of the black community. But this impression belies an exciting and dynamic story that may not be apparent to the casual observer.

As noted previously, the internal ritual life of the black church has empowered many adherents to enter the public arena in pursuit of a better society. The culture and public mission of most black churches remain in place; however, there is evidence of innovation. I would like to describe the innovations that I observed during a two-year research project on congregational life, which was supported by the Lilly Endowment.

Although this discussion should interest leaders and members of black churches, I think that its relevance extends far beyond that community. I firmly believe that the key to restoring urban civil society depends on the vitality of the faith community, including but not limited to black churches. For this reason, lessons learned in one community may help others seeking a way to contribute to the renewal of public life. Hence we all should pay attention to the new opportunities for and challenges to faith-based community transformation that have emerged in the past generation. Moreover, we should resolve to support communities of faith in this heroic quest. Consider, then, the following major themes that emerged during my investigation of change and continuity in black church culture since the civil rights movement.

> *I firmly believe that the key to restoring urban civil society depends on the vitality of the faith community.*

Declining Significance of Denominationalism

Prior to the civil rights movement, most people, black and white, took denominational identity quite seriously. This identity was often a marker of social mobility and part of the family social inheritance proudly passed on to successive generations. In 1996 the worship service for the presidential inauguration was held at a black church, the Metropolitan African Methodist Episcopal Church in Washington. There, the nation's most famous black preacher, Dr. Gardner Taylor, poked fun at denominational loyalties. He cited the adage that Methodists are Baptists who can read, Presbyterians are Methodists who have gone to college, and Episcopalians are Presbyterians whose investments have done well. This was a humorous and, I hope, nonoffensive way of characterizing what the theologian and social critic H. Richard Niebuhr had documented in his book, *The Social Sources of Denominationalism.*

Niebuhr noted that as Americans moved up in levels of education, wealth, and social status, they tended to change denominational identities—worshiping socially upward, if you will.

This pattern was common in black communities, although less dramatic in the years preceding the civil rights movement. During segregation, most black churches had members from a variety of social and educational levels worshiping together. Only the most affluent, and, typically, more assimilated, lighter-skinned blacks felt compelled to isolate themselves in enclaves of class and church that discriminated against blacks who didn't fit the preferred profile.

In addition to the congregational profile defined in terms of education, wealth, family name, skin complexion, region of origin, accent, and the like, certain liturgical practices became associated with lower-class religion, in contrast to the religion of the affluent class. For instance, the religion of assimilated blacks resembled that of whites. Typically, this included worship services that were brief and tightly orchestrated, and that included hymnals, organ music, sermons in lecture form, and little emphasis on money. In the black "folk" churches, however, one would find drums, guitars, tambourines, hand-clapping, foot-stomping, and even prescribed times and spaces for dancing and shouting. Services tended to be longer in duration, relaxed, and highly participatory with long sermons often concluded in a chanted cadence, and heavy emphasis on giving money.

When gospel geniuses like Thomas Dorsey, who wrote the classic song "Precious Lord," and Mahalia Jackson integrated drums and new rhythms into their emotionally liberating music, they were accused of embracing the devil's ways. Affluent blacks regarded such high-voltage religion with disdain, suspicion, and shame. Recall how W. E. B. Du Bois described his first visit to an outdoor revival among the poor black people of rural Tennessee:

> It was out in the country, far from home, far from my foster home, on a dark Sunday night. The road wandered from our rambling longhouse up the stony bed of a creek . . . until we could

hear dimly across the fields a rhythmic cadence of song—soft, thrilling, powerful, that swelled and died sorrowfully in our ears. I was a country school teacher then, fresh from the East, and had never seen a Southern Negro revival. . . . A sort of suppressed terror hung in the air and seemed to seize us—a pythian madness, a demonic possession, that lent a terrible reality to song and word.[1]

During the 1960s, dramatic changes began to unfold in the congregational culture of black churches. As black people embraced their African identities, they began to incorporate African religious practices into their liturgies. Some observers referred to this phenomenon as the re-Africanization of black Christianity. I characterize this process of retrieving African practices with the metaphor of being baptized in the Nile River, a redemptive process of reclaiming one's spiritual origins. Consequently, the energy of revival-style, folk religion began to emerge in black churches with conventional liturgical practices. C. Eric Lincoln and Lawrence Mamiya documented one example of this emergence in describing a "neo-Pentecostal" trend in some rapidly growing African Methodist Episcopal churches due, in part, to the emphasis on the ministry and activity of the Holy Spirit.

The pervasive emphasis on the Spirit in black church culture received a significant endorsement when Dr. James Forbes delivered the 1986 Lyman Beecher Lectures at Yale University, in which he focused on the Holy Spirit and preaching. Forbes argued that there has been a tragic and suspicious neglect of the third person of the Trinity in most contemporary theological discourse. By reflecting on the work of the Holy Spirit in our ministries, he continued, we may discover empowering resources for personal and social transformation. Forbes's appeal has been heeded, and today ministers from all sectors of the black Christian tradition speak freely about the presence and work of the Holy Ghost or Holy Spirit in their lives.

This baptism in the Nile provided an important turning point in black church culture for two reasons. First, it removed the stigma attached to revivalistic religion, so that upwardly mobile black people could remain in their churches of origin without feeling the need to switch "upward." Second, one could switch churches if necessary with less fear of being accused of disloyalty or disrespect toward the faith of one's ancestors.

One of the important factors that made it easy for many black professionals to remain in "Grandma's church" was the presence of a new black clergy, of which I'll have more to say in chapter 6. One of the best examples of this phenomenon is Bishop Charles Blake in Los Angeles. Although his West Angeles Church of God in Christ includes celebrities such as basketball star Magic Johnson and actor Denzel Washington among its six thousand members, Blake reminds them that his church represents part of the "holy roller" tradition that the affluent used to despise. Ministers like Blake even attracted people from Catholic and mainline Protestant congregations; hence, it became possible to switch "downward" without losing status among one's peers. This strikes me as an extraordinary development. By the 1970s and 1980s it became common, as it is today, to see young black professionals attending Baptist and Pentecostal congregations where emotionally liberated worship is the norm.

If denominational affiliation now matters less than it previously did, certainly the characteristics of individual congregations matter a great deal to younger churchgoers. In our investigation of Atlanta megachurches, 23 percent of the members of Antioch Baptist Church had been members of other denominations, with a majority of that group having come from Methodist and Catholic congregations. Sixty-seven percent of respondents at the Cathedral of Faith Church of God in Christ had belonged to other denominations, with 41.9 percent having come from the Baptist church and 6.2 percent from Methodist congregations. It appears that black parishioners have become congregational consumers, using a shopping list of desired characteristics when searching for a church

> *Black parishioners have become congregational consumers, using a shopping list of desired characteristics when searching for a church home.*

home. The list includes the vibrancy of its worship and music, spiritually fulfilling and intellectually stimulating preaching, safety and attractiveness of the church environment, quality programs for children, programs for single people, and the convenient scheduling of worship services.

If churches in decline are able to adjust some congregational practices in order to appeal to the church consumers, it could be good for the churches and for people who genuinely seek a church community. One of the dangers of this phenomenon, however, is that churches may compromise the integrity of the gospel they proclaim and forsake the rich modes of worship that distinguish them as members of a particular tradition.

Church and Community Conflict

One of the frustrating challenges faced by congregations remaining in inner-city neighborhoods is the attempt to achieve good relations with the surrounding neighborhood. Harvard sociologist William Julius Wilson has written several influential books about the changes that occurred in urban black communities after the civil rights movement. He underscores that poorer and unemployed blacks are now both physically and culturally isolated from the large majority of middle-class and affluent blacks. Upwardly mobile blacks who move from central-city neighborhoods to the suburbs often break all ties to the previous community. For many, the only remaining connection to the old neighborhood is the church they attend. We interviewed black professionals who drove forty-five minutes to one hour to get to their family church.

The picture of affluent blacks driving attractive vehicles into impoverished neighborhoods once a week, while making little contact with local residents, is disturbing. Many residents resent the relative wealth of fellow church members and express it by vandalizing automobiles and church property. Pastors commonly have to replace broken windows and stolen public-address equipment. Back at St. Paul Church in Chicago, just two blocks from the largest low-income housing development in the nation (Robert Taylor Homes), we replaced stolen microphones several times before building a tall fence around the church and installing an electronic security system. In every major city in the country one hears stories of churches that have done the same.

The prospect of losing church members afraid to attend an inner-city congregation has prompted many pastors to begrudgingly "fortify" the church with fences, security systems, dogs, and, in some cases, armed guards. When I asked a deacon at a local church how he justified the presence of armed patrolmen, he replied that they were merely stewards of God's church preventing the forces of hell from prevailing.

I describe this as "inner-city Christian realism," picking up on Reinhold Niebuhr's recognition that Christians may feel compelled to undertake actions that are less than ideal, even tragic, for the sake of preventing a greater evil. Pastors and church members recognize the contradiction of having to "lock down" the church as they drive away from the neighborhood after services, but see no realistic, responsible alternative.

One of the most hopeful developments has occurred in Boston. Stunned and outraged when gang members, guns blazing, stormed a local church during a funeral for a teenager, neighborhood clergy and church members organized street patrols, which evolved into a comprehensive social service and community development ministry for youths involved in gangs, their families, and affected neighborhoods. Known as the Ten-Point Coalition, the group now receives foundation, corporate, and individual support to undertake a range of preventative ministries.

The Afrocentric Aesthetic

Since the civil rights era, many parishioners and clergy have sought a variety of ways to express pride in their African identities. During the height of the movement, African Americans began to wear African clothing along with natural and "Afro" hairstyles, and to decorate their homes with African art. Many black families adopted the Kwanzaa holiday and began to learn words from ki-Swahili, commonly spoken in eastern Africa. But for several years most black churches shied away from incorporating explicitly African art or rituals into their worship culture.

Younger, seminary-educated clergy exposed to black liberation theology began to press the issue in their local congregations. During the 1970s and 1980s, more churches began to place African art in the sanctuary. Many began to adopt "African dress days" when all parishioners were urged to wear African clothing. Churches began to sponsor tourist visits to Africa and to pay more attention to the plight of African peoples, especially to the anti-apartheid struggle in South Africa. To express a more permanent and personal identification with Africa, a small number of blacks adopted African names.

One of the most controversial expressions of new black pride in the congregational culture was the removal or alteration of paintings, stained glass, statues, and icons depicting Jesus and other holy figures as people of European descent. Most older African Americans had been acculturated to accept such famous depictions as Warner Sallman's "Head of Christ" as normative. Most of them did not regard this traditional art as offensive or noteworthy. Younger blacks, however, who were influenced by Malcolm X and other black nationalist leaders, adamantly rejected these images. For instance, the Nation of Islam published a one-page announcement with a photo of a black-skinned, crucified Jesus. The caption read, "If white people were forced to stare at this for 400 years, what would it do to their minds?"

Installing a new Afrocentric aesthetic has been a slow and difficult process for many black churches. One young pastor reports that, upon his appointment, he noticed a huge painted statue of a white Jesus behind the choir stand. Without consultation he removed it. On Sunday, members were so upset the image had been moved that they could not worship. He says that the congregation decided to have a candid conversation about the issue.

Together they reached a compromise: the statue would be restored, and a professional artist would be hired to paint it to resemble a suntanned Palestinian Jew. Another pastor noted that he had a major challenge to replace the stained-glass windows, which all depicted the white founders of the denomination. He was concerned about the ability of the church to attract new members given the prominence of the culturally inappropriate art. The church decided to replace the original glass panes with new ones, showing the black founders of the denomination. It was a long-term, expensive process that eventually satisfied everyone. The incident shows clearly that baby-boomer blacks feel empowered to interpret and create sacred images and art in ways that did not occur to their parents. It took a cultural revolution in black America's sense of its own beauty and value in order to authorize the exciting developments underway throughout black church culture.

> *Baby-boomer blacks feel empowered to interpret and create sacred images and art in ways that did not occur to their parents.*

Another exciting development in the Afrocentric aesthetic movement involves a new "village" architecture that seeks to create African-style religious spaces. This is evident in the open, round, theater-like spaces of the Brentwood Baptist Church in Houston; the Trinity United Church of Christ in Chicago; and the Light of the World Christian Church in Indianapolis. I expect that this trend will continue as younger pastors begin to build new sanctuaries.

It should be noted that black churches have met in all sorts of spaces. Typically, the upwardly mobile congregations moved forward in at least three stages. First, as blacks migrated from the South to the North earlier this century, they were content to rent or buy storefront property in order to establish themselves in the community. Later, in a second stage, some congregations were able to purchase sanctuaries formerly used by white congregations. Blacks often modified those spaces to make them more user-friendly. A third stage involved those churches that had the rare opportunity to build a new church building. Now there are many architects, engineers, and artists who can help local churches to make culturally appropriate choices.

Exposing Gender Tensions

Most discussions about gender and the black church focus on the mixed experience of men in organized religion, noting that male clergy tend to benefit from church affiliation while laymen both love and hate it. But there is an important and exciting story to be told of the emergence of women in ministry, theological education, and leadership in society. Fortunately, numerous observers and leaders of the black church are doing that work, including scholars such as Prathia Hall, Daphne Wiggans, and Joy Browne. To be sure, as the African American community strives to promote a culture that supports healthy marriages and families, the church will continue to play a lead in reclaiming and transforming disaffected men into productive citizens and family members.

In our survey at the 1992 Hampton University Ministers Conference, a part of the Lilly project, we discovered that 61 percent of the responding clergy had a program to attract more men to church. Although affirmed as worthwhile projects, the programs raise the concern of many women who regard them as subtle efforts to reestablish patriarchal power and privilege in the church. Movements such as the 1995 Million Man March and Promise Keepers raise as much anxiety as hope for some women. Some feminist and womanist leaders show concern that male reclamation could subvert the rising aspirations of women for equal treatment before the law and altar.

Many of us believe that God intends women and men to be partners in ministry. It is now time to make this a policy for our churches. Although progress toward this goal will play out differently in each tradition, the ethical mandate for inclusiveness must be on the agenda of all our churches. We also need to celebrate and to develop more models of partnership that affirm men while respecting women's talents, rights, and opportunities.

The struggle for gender justice in American churches has been waged on several fronts—individual, familial, congregational, denominational, and societal. At each level, advocates of and those resistant to change collide over the same basic issues. If we dissect the major sources of conflict, it seems that four dimensions have been most prominent: moral, political, economic, and cultural.

The *moral* dimension of the struggle pertains to biblical and theological questions surrounding the issue. Does God call women into ministry? What does the Bible say about the issue? Should churches seek to prevent women from engaging in pastoral ministry? Does God approve of churches that fight over this issue?

> *We need to celebrate and to develop more models of partnership that affirm men while respecting women's rights, talents, and opportunities.*

The *political* dimension relates to questions of power, authority, and control of ecclesiastical privilege. Many men resist women's ordination because they do not want to share or relinquish this control. Also, many women who have been socialized to accept ministry as a male vocation oppose extending this privilege to other women. Unsurprisingly, some people frame their political resistance in biblical and theological terms. This complicates what ought to be a straightforward issue. Even when the layer of resistance based on the Bible is engaged, peeled away, and set aside, very human anxiety over loss of control often clouds rational discourse.

The *economic* dimension appears when people speculate about the likely impact of women's presence in ministry on male clergy compensation and benefits. I have discovered that this dimension of the debate often does not receive explicit attention, although privately, clergy admit that it is a real concern. To my knowledge, there has been no careful study of the economic impact of women in ministry on male earnings. However, one could infer from the experience of women who have entered previously male-dominated professions that the market generally rewards excellence and tends to discourage or drive out mediocrity. Men who have valuable ministries should not feel threatened by women seeking to uplift the community. Indeed, we should replace this zero-sum paradigm with a more hopeful vision that acknowledges the masses of unchurched people and resources that remain untapped.

The *cultural* dimension of the debate pertains to popular images, expectations, and stereotypes of what a minister should look like. Ministers have symbolic power. That power has been gained through long years of tradition and habit. No matter how much, or how little, charisma a clergyperson might possess, she or he participates in the power of the holy that the tradition has cultivated. Although this power has eroded in our secularizing culture, for many communities it remains a considerable force. In black church culture, the power of the minister is an exceedingly important factor which explains why ministry remains a respected calling. But like the larger culture in which it took shape, black church culture has viewed pastoral ministry as a calling for males only. Efforts by women to transform that assumption must work at this deep level of cultural and individual psychology.

The movement for equal opportunity in ministry has accelerated since the 1970s as more women have gone to seminary and graduated with hopes of employment. In our Hampton Ministers Survey, 68.1 percent of the clergy respondents, who were predominantly male, categorically supported equal opportunity for women in ministry. Another 17.5 percent expressed qualified support. Only 7 percent were opposed.

It seems that at least four major factors contribute to the momentum behind this important struggle for justice and inclusion. First, women in ministry have succeeded. Many who doubted the legitimacy of female ordained clergy and pastors thought that women's failure would validate their own resistance. However, some of the most dynamic and prophetic ministries and megachurches are led by women. For example, Rev. Dr. Vashti McKenzie, the leader of Payne Memorial African Methodist Episcopal Church in Baltimore, exemplifies a class of black female pastors who have developed vital ministries for the entire family, attracted and retained men, and been forceful and effective advocates for gender justice within and outside the African Methodist Episcopal tradition. Her book *Not Without a Struggle* provides helpful lessons for effective pastoral leadership and coping strategies for women (and men) in ministry.[2] Dr. McKenzie, whom many predict will become the African Methodist Episcopal denomination's first elected bishop, is just one among scores of effective female pastors. A few whom I have come to know include Dr. Susan Johnson Cook formerly of the Mariner's Temple Baptist Church in New York; Dr. Johnnie Coleman of the Christ Universal Temple in Chicago; Dr. Barbara King of the Hillside Truth Center, Dr. Romani L. Howard of the New Hope Church of God in Christ, and Dr. Cynthia Hale of the Ray of Hope Christian Church, all in Atlanta.

Although many biblical passages on superficial reading seem to place limits on the public ministry of women, mature believers are called to read the text in context and with deeper spiritual insight into the character of God. One of the passages that has been important in helping men and women to keep an open mind is Acts 5:33-39. In this narrative, the apostles are apprehended for preaching the gospel and brought before a council of rabbis for interrogation and punishment. In defense of Peter, Gamaliel, a Pharisee "held in respect by all the people," urges the rabbis to "keep away from these men and let them alone; for if this plan or this work is of men, it will come to nothing. But if it is of God, you cannot overthrow it—lest you even be found to fight against God." Gamaliel's words have become a wonderfully pragmatic test relevant to other innovations in the church. So the success of women in pastoral and other ordained ministries presents weighty evidence of God behind the movement. Like Jackie Robinson, the first black player in major league baseball, these women have passed the test of readiness and effectiveness with flying colors.

> *The success of women in pastoral and other ordained ministries presents weighty evidence of God behind the movement.*

A second advance for women's presence in ministry has been the publication of an impressive literature analyzing gender roles in the church. Of course, all scholars have political loyalties and agendas, and their writings must be read critically. Reading critically includes placing the author's perspective in dialogue with other sources: the Bible, church tradition, human reason, the social sciences, common human experience, and the wisdom of the community's elders.

Among those who have ably documented the exemplary ministerial and lay leadership of African American church women and provided biblical, historical, theological, and practical perspectives on women's full participation in ministry are Dr. Cheryl Townsend Gilkes of Colby College; Dr. Evelyn Brooks Higgenbotham of Harvard Divinity School; Dr. Prathia Hall of United Theological Seminary; Dr. Cheryl Sanders of the Howard University School of Divinity; Dr. Marcia Riggs of Columbia Theological Seminary; Dr. Jacquelyn Grant of the Interdenominational Theological Center; Dr. Renita Weems of Vanderbilt Divinity School; and Dr. Delores Williams of Union Theological Seminary. Their books and others have provided essential intellectual capital for clarifying the church's theology and practice as denominations have discussed the topic.

The third significant factor advancing the cause of women in ministry has been the conversion and supportive advocacy of prominent male ministers. In light of the influence exercised by "elders" in black church culture, the endorsement of respected, successful, and saintly male preachers goes a long way toward setting aside some of the political, biblical, economic, and cultural resistance identified above. Several male clergy from traditions that have not officially ordained women have encountered retaliation from their peers and leaders. Dr. H. Beecher Hicks of the Metropolitan Baptist Church in Washington notes that after partici-

> *The endorsement of respected, successful, and saintly male preachers goes a long way toward setting aside some of the political, biblical, economic, and cultural resistance to women in ministry.*

pating in ordination ceremonies for women he was voted out of the local Baptist Ministers Conference. Bishop Ozro T. Jones of the Church of God in Christ (Philadelphia) has also been stigmatized by peers in the denomination for ordaining women. Despite pressure, these pastors have inspired proteges to be open-minded and accepting of their female peers. When theological ethicist Katie Cannon became the first African American woman ordained by the Presbyterian Church (USA), she notes that she was affirmed by men.

The fourth significant factor has been the example set by some black denominations. Among the major historically black denominations, it appears that the first to ordain a woman was the Christian Methodist Episcopal Church in the early 1900s. The African Methodist Episcopal Church began ordaining women in the 1940s. The Progressive National Baptist Convention has ordained women since its founding in 1961. Smaller denominations such as the United Holy Church of America have ordained woman since the end of the nineteenth century. Some women ordained by mainline denominations have ascended to episcopal office, including Bishop Leontine Kelly (United Methodist Church) and Bishop Barbara Harris (Episcopal Church). Although at the outset most of these traditions moved forward cautiously, they did move forward with a sense of God's leading and have become stronger.

The Decline of Black Folk Preaching

J. Irwin Miller, an authority on homiletics, has identified three major traditions of preaching in North America: Puritan, evangelical, and Pentecostal.[3] The Puritan tradition is represented by Lyman Beecher and the New England clerics who sought to address the human intellect with the goal of enhancing human enlightenment about God. The evangelical preaching tradition, best represented by Billy Graham, aims at the human heart or soul to convince people of their sinfulness and to lead them to a personal conversion. The Pentecostal tradition addresses the human spirit, seeking to evoke praise in awareness of the presence and glory of God.

The most engaging preachers, such as Martin Luther King, tend to combine these traditions to address the multiple needs of their listeners. Historically, black folk preaching has been a communal practice in which the people have dialogue with the preacher and with God. Worshipers have expected sermons to be poetic masterpieces that are biblically rooted, politically prophetic, intellectually stimulating, emotionally evocative, rhetorically polished, pastorally sensitive, and reverently and joyfully delivered. This was the norm when people were acquainted with common biblical stories and language.

Examples of this preaching tradition can be found in collections of black sermons.[4] Still, my favorite source for appreciating the magic of black sacred rhetoric is the fiction and poetry of Zora Neale Hurston and James Weldon Johnson. Many people are acquainted with the title of Johnson's famous book, *God's Trombones*, but may not be aware that this collection of poems is based on sermons by folk preachers in rural Florida. Similarly, Hurston's wonderful novel, *Jonah's Gourd Vine*, depicts a well-meaning but often errant preacher who ultimately seeks to redeem himself through preaching. In chapter 2, I included a large excerpt from Hurston's novel that illustrates the beauty and power of the language.

One of the most distinctive features of black folk preaching, differentiating it from other preaching cultures is the practice of concluding a sermon in a chanted, musical manner known as *hooping*. The practice has proven controversial among younger, well-educated black parishioners and clergy. My seminary students used to debate whether the practice should be discontinued. Participants in the Hampton survey, when asked, "How do you feel about the practice of hooping?" showed that it still has support. Fifty-three percent said they supported hooping; 11 percent were opposed. Twenty-six percent said they were indifferent. When asked, "Do you hoop?" 53 percent said they did so occasionally, while 34 percent said never. Only 4 percent said they always used hooping in the sermon.

Although more than half of the respondents supported hooping, anecdotal evidence gleaned from other clergy and parishioners suggests that it is very controversial and is regarded contemptuously by younger, well-educated churchgoers. This mixed support places many seminarians and future members of the clergy in a dilemma. While wanting to communicate effectively with all segments of the black community, they recognize that preferences in rhetorical practice differ significantly among the affluent elite and the working class and poor masses. Most of these clergy end up bilingual and seek to apply their dual competencies in their appropriate contexts.

Traditional folk preaching—a style both beloved and despised—may be at a crossroad. Although many older worshipers familiar with the tradition continue in their support, many younger worshipers show that they are drawn to a very different style of sermon delivery and worship. The new style entails a more lecture-like teaching of biblical truths, aimed at building the personal faith of the believer. It is common among congregations known as word churches for their emphasis on teaching only the word of God.

The Rise of Word Churches and the Teaching Sermon

The word-church phenomenon emerges from the predominantly white evangelical community but includes charismatic and Pentecostal ministers as well. Nationally known televangelists such as Kenneth Hagin, Kenneth Copeland, and Jimmy Swaggart have spread the appeal of biblical exposition and exhortation. In the black community, the better-known examples of word theology and preaching include Rev. Fred Price of Los Angeles, Rev. Creflo Dollar of Atlanta, Rev. John Cherry of Maryland, and Rev. Anthony Evans of Dallas. The Reverend Cherry, whom President Clinton has affirmed in a State of the Union address, is the pastor of an African Methodist Episcopal Zion Church with more than twenty thousand members.

I offer the four observations about this movement. First, independent word churches represent an alternative to conventional black Christianity. In a market-dominated culture, that such new spiritual expressions would flourish is unremarkable. That they are growing rapidly raises questions about the kind of religion that they offer, and the value or utility of such faith for fulfilling the historical spiritual and social agenda of black churches. Second, word churches are not monolithic but encompass considerable variety, including Full Gospel Baptists, neo-Pentecostal Methodists, traditional evangelicals, and some mainline congregations. Third, word churches that proselytize aggressively may attract large numbers of members who seek a more engaged, demanding form of Christian faith. This is likely to place them in tension with the mainline churches in the black community. Fourth, word churches that proclaim the gospel of health, wealth, and success through personal acts of heroic faith (similar to the grassroots revivalist tradition described in chapter 2) may be guilty of distorting the explicit message of the Christian tradition. For instance, by making human will and the exercise of personal faith equal with the mysterious and omnipotent intentions of God, these churches may unwittingly disempower God and enthrone themselves as the arbiters of divine will. Word-church leaders thereby stand in danger of exalting themselves as exceptional messengers of the divine mysteries, and of cultivating the dependence of followers anxious to master the secret formulae for quick prosperity, and freedom from illness and anxiety.

Younger parishioners dissatisfied with traditional black church worship have flocked to these congregations, many of which are now megachurches. These churches tend to deemphasize the role and value of the historically black denominations, preferring to promote a more individualistic style of faith based on biblical teachings. Word-church ministers tend not to focus on social evils such as racism, sexism, and class discrimination, nor to mobilize members to counteract these forces. Rather they tend to spiritualize these sins, urging members not to engage personally in such behavior.

Word-church ministers have been very effective in using radio, television, audio and video tapes, and the Internet in communicating their message. Their seeming omnipresence in various media formats suggests that the word-church community may be larger than it really is. More significant than their number is the influence this method of preaching has on the traditional black church. Recognizing the appeal of substantive presentations for younger worshipers, and frustrated by the swelling biblical illiteracy in the community at large, more and more black preachers are adopting this method. Even in the Pentecostal church that my research team observed, we noted that the minister focused less on evoking praise and ecstasy and more on implanting Bible stories, moral values, and Christian rituals that Sunday school had accomplished for earlier generations.

Although I can affirm the word church's focus on Bible study and teaching, I am concerned about its long-term impact on two features of traditional black folk preaching: the poetry and the justice agenda. It would be a loss to Christendom and to the English language if the poetry and art of black preaching yielded to cultural pressures to make it more cognitive and discursive. Preaching is not philosophical argumentation but an invitation to take an imaginative journey, to visit ancient places, and to overhear the conversations of Moses, Esther, and Jesus. As it engages the imagination, effective preaching moves deep into the human psyche and can lead to new ways of seeing the world, to decisions to change direction in life, and to new encounters with the holy. The flat language of the lecture cannot do that.

> Preaching is not philosophical argumentation but an invitation to take an imaginative journey, to visit ancient places, and to overhear the conversations of Moses, Esther, and Jesus.

We should also remember that the black church in America came into existence because of the nation's serious race problem. I believe that the birth of the black church was a gift from God to a nation in denial of its own sins; God wanted America to have a conversion experience. Given the slow and complicated workings of national redemption, the eradication of racism through legislation, education, and conversion still has a long way to go. Consequently, black churches cannot give up on their original mission until it is complete. Similarly, white, Latino, Asian, and Native American churches must fulfill their responsibility to invite and lead their communities out of denial, toward repentance and renewal.

Whether the word-church phenomenon continues as the exciting and rapidly growing movement that we have witnessed during the 1980s and 1990s remains to be seen. Should these churches continue to grow, however, other believers must hold them accountable for their divergence from authentic Christian theology. Only through dialogue can a challenge be raised to three errors I have noted among some of the movement's leaders and churches: (1) an imbalanced biblical hermeneutic that focuses on individual faithfulness at the expense of social justice; (2) inhospitality toward other Christians and deep suspicion toward anything ecumenical; and (3) indifference toward the history and living legacy of the black Christian liberation struggle.

We should note finally that part of the appeal of the word church (and other one-dimensional religious expressions) is that it provides simple answers to life's toughest questions, offers practical advice and rules for living, and provides rich social interaction with other positive individuals in a warm, affirming atmosphere. If mainline churches are to compete in the marketplace of religious seekers, they must become more savvy in using radio and television to present their message while improving the quality of their liturgical culture to include lively worship and supportive programs for families.

Innovations in Congregational Culture

One of the most exciting developments in the emerging black church is the presence of dynamic, smart, spiritually mature, articulate leaders who are ushering in change. Most are products of the black liberation theology movement that swept through graduate theological education during the 1970s and 1980s. More than any other theologian, James H. Cone of the Union Theological Seminary in New York provided the intellectual leadership for this movement. Cone has fused the theological and political visions and analysis of Martin Luther King and Malcolm X with categories from Western Christian theology to make his project appropriate for a graduate theological curriculum. Cone's own writings are voluminous, numbering more than twenty books. His vision of a renewed black church and clergy has also been amplified by his many students holding teaching positions in the nation's leading seminaries.

Pastors trained in black liberation theology have initiated the following kinds of innovation. First, one can see *change in the worship culture of the new black church*. Increasing numbers of congregations now offer multiple worship services to accommodate the different work schedules of parishioners. The Trinity United Church in Chicago has instituted an informal-dress service on Saturday evening. An increasing number of churches have developed services one and a half hours in length. The West Angeles Church of God in Christ in Los Angeles has four services every Sunday morning; the last is more traditional and relaxed and usually runs well over two hours. Glide Memorial United Methodist Church in San Francisco sometimes conducts worship services featuring a rock band, overhead projection of hymn lyrics, and dancing in the aisles.

Some congregations are seeking to integrate new musical styles into worship. For instance, Rev. Dr. C. Dexter Wise of Ohio has recorded gospel rap songs in which he seeks to spread the gospel to a younger generation. Unlike many of the young gospel rap artists on the scene today, ministers like Dr. Wise are acquainted with the history of the freedom struggle tradition in the black church and can educate younger people regarding this noble history of socia l gospel activism.

More congregations are seeking to nurture a plurality of musical forms within the worship culture. Most churches—like Trinity United Church of Christ in Chicago—accomplish this aim by maintaining several choirs devoted to specific genres of music, such as spirituals, popular gospel, traditional hymns, and classical or baroque, and present all of these forms regularly. Professionally trained music directors are bringing new breadth and vitality to traditional church music. Many of these directors have studied with masters such as the late Dr. Wendell Whalum of Morehouse College, who also taught thousands of music directors at the Hampton Ministers Conference, and Dr. Melva Costen, the Helmar Emil

Nielsen Professor of Music and Worship at the Interdenominational Theological Center, which has produced a steady supply of accomplished church musicians.

Second, there have been fascinating *innovations in traditional weekly Bible study sessions.* Increasingly, churches are moving beyond the model in which one person makes a presentation to a passive group of listeners and are using audiovisual equipment to make biblical materials come alive. Drs. John Grayson and Teena Johnson-Smith of Mount Holyoke College encourage professors to use of multimedia resources in teaching classical texts. Professor Grayson juxtaposes text, music, and video materials in courses that seek to present multiple perspectives on topics such as crucifixion and exodus.

Churches that, during Bible study or worship, wish to emphasize the African presence in the Bible can now draw upon an extensive set of materials. Books by leading black biblical scholars such as Charles Copher (ITC), Cain Hope Felder (Howard University), Renita Weems (Vanderbilt), and the seminar group that produced *Stony the Road We Trod* are helping to enrich resources for Christian education. It is popular now for congregations to read the work of these leading scholars and then to invite the scholar to the church for lectures, preaching, and further discussion.

A third significant feature of renewed congregations is the number of *specialized ministries for various life cycle and interest groups.* For young adults returning to church after marriage and/or the birth of their first child, a comfortable nursery and other child-friendly ministries are very important in securing their loyalty. With increasing numbers of African Americans postponing marriage, many single people are searching for a social life congruent with their faith commitments. Congregations, either through the services of a consultant or their own self-assessment, would do well to explore how their culture and environment invite or repel children, young adults, and single people.

> *Congregations would do well to explore how their culture and environment invite or repel children, young adults, and single people.*

Another fascinating innovation in black church culture is the *increased use of media*, both to disseminate information and to nurture spiritual growth and faith development. A significant number of African American churchgoers use audio and video tapes to strengthen their faith commitments. Often they are urged by pastors who believe church attendance once or twice a week inadequate for immersing a believer in the word of God.

The same holds true for people preparing for ministry. Dr. Gardner Taylor has suggested that one wishing to become a great preacher should listen to great preachers. It is common for ministers to listen to recorded sermons and lectures while driving or going about their daily responsibilities. While in seminary, I used to take walks while carrying a tape recorder and tapes of C. L. Franklin (Aretha Franklin's father), Gardner Taylor, Jasper Williams, Howard Thurman, Bishop Samuel Crouch, Malcolm X, and Yvonne Delk. Each offered theological and ethical insights and political analyses using compelling rhetorical strategies, which had an impact on my emerging vision and voice.

Aware of a large market for religious media, talented and entrepreneurial preachers have produced sermons and lectures sold at national denominational meetings and annual conferences. One of my favorite lecture series is "Hoopology" by Rev. Jasper Williams, pastor of Salem Baptist Church in Atlanta. Williams is concerned that as more ministers learn homiletics in graduate seminaries, fewer learn about hooping, the folk art discussed earlier of delivering the sermon (especially its conclusion) in a chanted, musical style. His practical "how-to-hoop" tape offers tips on preserving this dimension of oral culture in the black church.

According to the American Association for the Advancement of Science, which has conducted limited research in this area, between 15 and 30 percent of black churches in certain localities operate radio or television stations, or purchase radio or television time to propagate religious messages. The association has been interested in the potential of existing radio ministries to promote science and math literacy among young people.

Building on this fascinating hunch, the Institute of Church Administration and Management at ITC is engaged in a two-year study of African American religious broadcasting to determine the number of broadcasts and the nature of this rapidly growing field. One of the important issues that they are exploring is the social consciousness and moral agenda of the most influential and popular clergypersons in the media. Already their investigations confirm my sense that a content analysis of the televangelists' message indicates an almost exclusive concern with the individual believer's ability to manage his or her affairs and to be healthy, wealthy, and successful.

Challenges and Opportunities

The Unchurched

Past studies of black church attendance have noted the highest rates of unchurched (nonattending, nonaffiliated) African Americans among northern, urban, young, less-educated males. I have seen neither scientific nor anecdotal evidence to counter this observation. Indeed, I observed the large and apparently growing unchurched youth population when I lived in Chicago, Boston, and Rochester, New York. By contrast, after moving to Atlanta we encountered a culture in which church membership and attendance were publicly discussed and approved. In view of changes in the economy—such as the increasing necessity of higher education for participation in the labor force—and growing despair about the future, I predict that the number of unchurched African Americans will continue to increase, particularly among the urban poor, who are already isolated from middle-class black America. Their needs will test the capacity of the historic black church to serve those who have no relationship with, or orientation to, its culture.

> *The needs of the unchurched will test the capacity of the historic black church to serve those who have no relationship with, or orientation to, its culture.*

Non-Christian Traditions

C. Eric Lincoln and Lawrence Mamiya's research on the growth of African American Muslim communities suggests tremendous vitality and a promising future. Although the Nation of Islam is the most visible non-Christian expression in the black community, it is relatively small in relation to the more orthodox American Muslim Mission led by Elijah Muhammad's son, Imam Warith D. Muhammad of Chicago. Nevertheless, for most African Americans, Islam is whatever the Nation of Islam practices and believes. This is an unfortunate assumption because it neglects the varieties of vibrant Muslim faith in North America.

Although Islam seems to be experiencing significant growth, with attractive, expensive mosques appearing throughout urban America, as a tradition it does not seem to pose a threat to the numbers or size of traditional black churches. Few Christians are leaving their churches through conversions to Islam. Even Benjamin Chavis's affiliation with the Nation of Islam has not generated a flow of followers. As an aggregate, Muslim communities in the black community would probably compare in size to one of the medium-sized black denominations, with between one million and three million believers.

The growing Muslim presence does represent a challenge to the moral agenda of traditional black churches. Although generally similar, there are differences in the Muslim and Christian agendas that could challenge the churches. For instance, some Muslim communities discourage explicitly political behavior and pay greater attention to personal moral renewal. Many black churches share this orientation. But many African Americans also admire the personal discipline and public displays of spirituality evident among some Muslims. This could place subtle pressure on church leaders to incorporate a more apolitical perspective into their ministries. The same concern could be raised with regard to the status of women in some Muslim traditions. But it is important to emphasize the considerable variety within and between differing Muslim traditions, and it is just as unfair to generalize about *the* Muslim perspective as to make claims about *the* Christian perspective.

Other non-Christian traditions are numerous, with particular strength in some regions. For instance, one can find African American Hebrew communities in Chicago, New York, and Miami. Traditional African religions are being practiced in many urban centers throughout the United States. Yoruba religion seems to be growing in popularity among better-educated black nationalists. Traditions popular throughout the Caribbean, such as Santería and voodoo, have adherents among immigrant communities on the East Coast. Yet despite the expanding menu of religious options in the black community, none approaches Islam in size or in its attractiveness to large numbers of African Americans.

African American Catholics

In a wonderful history, Cyprian Davis notes that there are more than 1.5 million black Catholics in the United States, with the "major centers still being southern Louisiana and the metropolitan areas of New York, Chicago, Washington, D.C., Miami, and Los Angeles."[5] Despite their large numbers, he observes that "too long have black Catholics been anonymous."

In 1987 the Black Catholic Clergy Caucus convened for what became a milestone in the history of black Catholics. Black priests reckoned there with the racist past of the church and began to chart new directions and emphases for the good of black people and the entire Catholic Church. Since that meeting, several important events have occurred: the appointment of black bishops, a meeting with Pope John Paul II, and the production of important theological documents to guide significant reforms in black Catholic culture. Davis also notes that these reform energies were responsible, in part, for Father George Stallings's call for a "separate, semiautonomous status for black Catholics through the formation of an African American Rite," or ecclesiastical jurisdiction.

In view of the recent move by black Catholics to acknowledge and celebrate their distinctiveness, it would seem propitious for black Protestants and Catholics to increase dialogue, fellowship, and collaborative social action. For instance, black Catholic leaders have invested considerable time in developing documents and analyses of ethics and public policy, a concern shared by many Protestants. Both communities have a great deal to teach one another and will benefit from seizing the opportunity to get better acquainted.

New Black Clergy and Their Moral Agenda

Drawing on our Hampton University Ministers Conference survey, which formed part of the Lilly-funded project, I offer a sampling of clergy responses on various moral issues. Here, I present statistics on their answers to a variety of theological and moral questions and speculate about the significance of the responses, hoping to lay some groundwork for statements in the rest of the chapter, in which I also draw on survey information.

Among six hundred respondents, 70 percent were male; 20.7 percent were between thirty and forty years old, 35 percent between forty and fifty, and 22.7 percent between fifty and sixty. By region, 61.3 percent resided in the Northeast, 31.6 percent in the South, 3.8 percent in the Midwest, and 1.3 percent in the Far West. Those married with children accounted for 68.8 percent. With regard to education, 11 percent ended with a high school diploma; 11.4 percent earned college degrees; 22.5 percent had seminary degrees; and 37 percent had some form of nontheological postgraduate training.

Sexuality

Of the respondents, 79.3 percent said that they had taught about or preached a sermon on sexuality, with 85.3 percent having preached against premarital sex. A total of 77.1 percent had preached about homosexuality with 79 percent indicating their opposition.

Asked about the *Roe v. Wade* decision, the Supreme Court case permitting abortion until the age of fetal viability, 48.2 percent opposed the policy, 15.4 percent supported it categorically, and 27.7 percent supported it with qualifications.

A surprising 34.6 percent believed that AIDS is a divine curse. This response seemed to reflect the negative judgments about homosexuality, as well as frustration with the inability of science to discover a cure. I think that the response also signals the need for increased education about sexuality and disease transmission so that clergy and congregations do not inflict greater pain on the lives of people who are suffering and searching for empathy and care. Organizations such as the Balm in Gilead, which provide education about HIV/AIDS for the black church community, must intensify their efforts to reach black church leadership.

With regard to distributing condoms in public schools, 75.8 percent did not support the policy. This response may reflect the church's suspicion about value-neutral sex education. Given the high rates of teen pregnancy and disease, church leaders will need to grapple honestly with strategies for protecting young people from their own irresponsible behavior.

A total of 86.8 percent said that they would dedicate a baby born out of wedlock; 86.3 percent require some form of premarital counseling prior to performing a wedding.

In general, the responses on sexuality issues suggest that black clergy continue to be conservative in areas of family values and sexual ethics. The percentages on *Roe v. Wade* and dedication of babies suggest a strong belief in the clergy culture in new life as a sacred gift, notwithstanding the circumstances surrounding conception. But these numbers do not indicate the more complex reality common within congregations. Although the church publicly condemns certain behaviors and orientations, it privately expresses toleration and acceptance of those involved. Most pastors are acquainted with this complexity even as they go on record supporting the conservative values that are perceived as important for rebuilding the black family. At the same time as they express these views, they seek to exhibit love, mercy, and patience toward those at odds with cherished moral precepts. Just as the love ethic placed Jesus in tension, at times, with legal standards, a similar tension may confront contemporary pastors.

Politics

In responses to questions of political attitudes, 54.4 percent believed that preachers should run for political office; 83.1 percent believed it is appropriate during worship to urge people to register and to vote. Asked if Rev. Jesse Jackson should continue to run for the presidency, 32.6 percent said yes, 34.1 percent said no, and 27 percent were uncertain. Asked if another black person should run, 62.9 percent responded yes. Asked if they permitted politicians to address their congregations, 39.4 percent said yes, 44.6 percent said no, and 16 percent did not respond.[6]

While 82 percent supported Martin Luther King's nonviolent teachings, 30.6 percent owned a firearm. This fact seems to reflect the inner-city Christian realism that also appears within this chapter. Many clergy who embrace nonviolence as part of their strategy for social change regard violence in defense of the family as morally appropriate.

Economics

Asked if congregations should own their own businesses, 57.1 percent of the respondents said yes, 31.9 percent said no. Regarding church investment in the stock market or other ventures, 69.8 percent approved of such policies while 20 percent did not. This apparent openness to working within the market economy suggests that most black churches continue to regard themselves as agents for community development. (See chapter 6 for a list of organizations and opportunities to learn more about the church's role in economic improvement.)

Health

A total of 70.6 percent indicated that they took regular vacations; 73.8 percent get regular physical examinations; 57.1 percent participate regularly in recreational activities. While 89.3 percent believed in divine healing, 87.6 percent urge sick people to take medicine in addition to relying on prayer and faith. These responses suggest pragmatism among black clergy concerning the relationship

between faith and health. In Atlanta, the Carter Center, in cooperation with the Centers for Disease Control, provides instruction in
the relationship between religion and health, and the Morehouse
School of Medicine sponsors a joint master's degree with the Interdenominational Theological Center in public health and theology.

Race Relations

Asked if they had invited white ministers to preach in their pulpits,
52.4 percent of respondents said yes; 49.9 percent said they had
preached to a white congregation. A total of 63.4 percent regarded
interracial dialogue as very important, boding well for Cornel
West's call to renew the interracial coalition that existed during the
civil rights movement. Although 51.3 percent regarded interfaith
dialogue as very important, only 22 percent said they would permit
Louis Farrakhan to preach in their pulpits; 57.9 percent would not.
These responses suggest a cautious openness to dialogue with non-
Christian traditions. Groups such as the National Conference of
Christians and Jews in New York should seize the opportunity to
convene religious leaders for interfaith dialogue. Seminary educators may be encouraged to learn that 59.9 percent said they had
been influenced by black liberation theology, while 75.6 percent
had been influenced by black pride during the civil rights movement (compared to 64.3 percent in a study conducted by C. Eric
Lincoln and Lawrence Mamiya).

Winds of change indeed have blown through black churches.
Despite conservatism in many areas, they are also very dynamic
institutions. As they take on the internal and external challenges I
have mentioned, they will require insightful, creative leadership.
Are these leaders and communities of faith ready to address constructively the issues and challenges raised here? I believe that they
can be equipped and inspired to do more and to do better. In the
final chapter I will offer thoughts and suggestions concerning the
educational agenda needed to prepare clergy who wish to confront
the American crisis with hope.

4 EXODUS AND RETURN

Redeeming Prodigal Youths

As I recall the challenges of being an adolescent in an urban context, I know that I could not have survived without the support and love of an extended family, an engaging church, a network of caring neighbors, and mission-driven public school teachers and administrators. As I observe the current challenges facing adolescents, I worry that many do not have a similar "thick" network of care and discipline. I am particularly concerned about the role that churches are playing in the lives of young people.

Wasted Treasures

More and more people are discovering and despairing about the plight of young, urban, poor African American males in this society. Many feel compelled to improve their situation. An early warning signal appeared in the

December 1, 1986, issue of *Time*, which had a cover story titled, "Today's Native Sons: Inner-City Black Males Are America's Newest Lost Generation."[1] The authors found that although black men account for 6 percent of America's population, they make up half its male prisoners, and that the black male prison population exceeds the number of black men enrolled in college. When the national unemployment rate was 6.9 percent it was 15 percent for black men; for black teenage males it hovered near 40 percent. Unfortunately, in the past decade little has happened to change the melancholy prospects of these boys and men.

For many years scholars, public officials, and artists have sought to portray the predicament of "today's native sons" as a threat to the future of black families and neighborhoods and to the nation at large. Speaking to the annual convention of the American Psychological Association, Dr. Joseph N. Gayles, Jr., then vice president of the Morehouse School of Medicine, said, "It is important for our society to view black male health—both physical and mental—as a major public policy problem and address its solution as a social malignancy affecting . . . the very fabric of American society."[2] And, in his engaging and humorous keynote address at the National Prayer Breakfast in January 1997, renowned surgeon Dr. Ben Carson argued that the nation would be stronger and more secure if it could harness the contributions of black males. In the audience were President Clinton, Vice President Gore, several members of the Cabinet and Congress, as well as influential evangelical leaders Charles Colson (Prison Ministries), Pat Robertson ("700 Club"), and Bill Bright (Campus Crusade for Christ). The presence of these opinion leaders, listening to a young black male who had beaten the odds, was significant, because they have the capacity to urge middle-class, suburban America to show patience and generosity toward youth whom they generally regard as America's worst nightmare. Dr. Carson almost became one of the nation's "wasted treasures"—one of the young, angry black men with no stake in society. Instead, today he is an accomplished medical professional and a role model for countless people.

In a recent book, *Body Count: Moral Poverty and How to Win America's War against Crime and Drugs*, William J. Bennett, John J. DiIulio, Jr., and John P. Walters provide statistical support for a coming storm of youth crime and violence.[3] According to their demographic research the number of juveniles will increase substantially before 2010. While today there are "roughly 7.5 million boys ages 14 to 17," they write, "by the year 2000, there will be a million more people in that age bracket, half of them male. UCLA Professor James Q. Wilson predicts that 6 percent of these boys 'will become high rate, repeat offenders—thirty thousand more young muggers, killers, and thieves than we have now.' "[4]

Bennett and his coauthors refer to this segment of the youth population with the unfortunate label "superpredators" and suggest that they are "radically impulsive, brutally remorseless youngsters, including ever more preteenage boys, who murder, assault, rape, rob, burglarize, deal deadly drugs, join gun-toting gangs, and create serious communal disorders. Professor Wilson suggests that there are 'only two restraints on behavior—morality, enforced by individual conscience or social rebuke, and law, enforced by police and courts.' " The "superpredators" do not fear the stigma of arrest, the pains of imprisonment, or the pangs of conscience. They perceive hardly any relationship between doing right (or wrong) now and being rewarded (or punished) for it later. To these mean-street youngsters, the words *right* and *wrong* have no fixed moral meaning.[5] Although the criminologists' analysis refers to the entire youth population and should not be associated entirely with blacks, there is abundant evidence that young black males both perpetrate and are the victims of violent crime at much higher rates than other segments of the population.

Clearly America has reason for concern about the plight of its young people. The African American community has a particular obligation—indeed, an ethical imperative—to try to arrest the current trend of juvenile self-destruction. The church has a unique role as young people ask for assistance in getting their lives together.

In 1994 representatives of youth gangs from around the nation gathered in Kansas City for a gang peace summit. Dr. Mac Charles Jones, a Baptist pastor in the city, co-hosted the event at his church. Before his untimely death in 1997, Dr. Jones told me that the young leaders had come to him to ask for spiritual guidance. They wanted to know more about what religion could offer. Their desperate and earnest plea reminded me of the passage in Mary Shelley's *Frankenstein* in which the creature addresses his creator with stunning clarity and conviction. In these words, I can hear the pleadings and anguish of the boys in the 'hood as they confront the black middle class and the rest of affluent America.

> I am malicious because I am miserable. Am I not shunned and hated by all mankind? You, my creator, would tear me to pieces, and triumph; remember that and tell me why I should pity man more than he pities me? . . . I will revenge my injuries: if I cannot inspire love, I will cause fear; and chiefly towards you my arch-enemy . . . do I swear inextinguishable hatred. Have a care: I will work at your destruction, nor finish until I desolate your heart, so that you shall curse the hour of your birth.[6]

This haunting passage provides a call to action for the black middle class, which helped create these alienated youths but now has abandoned them, and now fears them. Many of these youths unwittingly prey on anyone who shows disrespect or who possesses material goods that they desire.

Crisis in Spiritual Identity

In my judgment, the core crisis that these wasted treasures face is *spiritual*. I use the term to refer to a person's sense of identity in relation to other people and to God. Rooted in spiritual identity are a person's fundamental values, moral commitments, and ability to engage in ethical reasoning. Spiritual health is reflected in a person's ability to trust and care for others. Spiritual people work actively to enhance life, love, truth, goodness, and beauty.

Behaviors that work against these goods manifest spiritual pathology.

The spiritual crisis facing America's troubled young people is not simply a problem internal to the individual, but also has complicated social dimensions. I have heard too many preachers condemning these young men without analyzing the circumstances that may frustrate any effort to improve their lives. These young men are not responsible for changes in the economy that affect their employment opportunities. Nor are they responsible for the poor quality of their neighborhood schools. Those concerned about these youth should avoid blaming them for conditions that are systemic. It is time to stop blaming the victims.

> *The high incidence of handgun violence, drug abuse, suicide, and spousal and child abuse should prompt us to ask what has occurred recently in the community to explain the rise of chaos and despair.*

The prodigal sons, however, are responsible for how they respond to, and manage, the hand that life has dealt. That is partly the message that the Million Man March sought to underscore, of which I will say more later. Black people faced difficult times in earlier days, but did not abandon all hope, personal dignity, collective purpose, or confidence in God. The high incidence of handgun violence, drug abuse, suicide, and spousal and child abuse should prompt us to ask what has occurred recently in the community to explain the rise of chaos and despair.

Sociologist William J. Wilson offers an important clue. He notes that

> In the mid-1960s, urban analysts began to speak of a *new dimension to the urban crisis* in the form of a large subpopulation of low-income families and individuals whose behavior contrasted sharply with the behavior of the general population. Despite a high rate of poverty in ghetto neighborhoods throughout the first half of the twentieth century, rates of inner-city joblessness, teenage pregnancies, out-of-wedlock births, female-headed fam-

lies, welfare dependency, and serious crime were significantly lower than in later years and did not reach *catastrophic proportions until the mid-1970s.*[7]

Wilson and others observe that the loss of high-wage, low-skill jobs for inner-city residents had a major impact on the economics and the culture of urban black neighborhoods. When the black middle class fled the inner cities (note that black flight followed white flight), the economic and cultural isolation of the urban poor deepened. Poor black people no longer had middle-class role models as neighbors or sources of information about job and educational opportunities. The underclass also lost models for presenting themselves in the work culture.

What will be done about this widening chasm in the black community between the haves and have-nots? I am persuaded that the churches have a critical role in empowering the poorest of the poor. This becomes more evident as the federal government seeks to shift responsibility for the provision of human services to state and local agencies.

But are the churches ready to undertake ministries that will effectively address the challenges facing young people, especially men? According to Drs. C. Eric Lincoln and Lawrence Mamiya, they are not. In *The Black Church in the African American Experience* Lincoln and Mamiya note that most black churches are doing poorly at providing engaging ministries for young people within the congregations, not to mention youths in the community who do not attend church.

Pastors admit that they need assistance in developing and implementing a new menu of programs for young members and for other youth in the neighborhood. Young people indicate that they find church services boring and irrelevant to their experience. Their dissatisfaction echoes some of the concerns expressed to me during field research for my master's thesis at Harvard Divinity School. After outlining some sources of dissatisfaction with the church I will consider some innovative programs with promise for attracting and retaining young people in church-based programs.

Crisis of Institutional Participation

Considering evidence showing high unemployment and school dropout rates, low marriage rates, and comparatively low church attendance rates for black males, we can postulate a crisis of male participation in the institutions responsible historically for social-izing members of the community. There appears to be at least a fourfold disengagement from institutional commitments to school, work, family, and church. Since I am not familiar with all of the social-scientific data on the social behavior of black males, I want to be cautious about advancing these ideas about nonpartici-pation. However, in my travels and interviews of church leaders and scholars, I am persuaded that these claims have some merit.

At Morehouse College, I was one of a small group of students who attended church regularly. On Sunday mornings the dormito-ries were deathly silent compared to the frivolity of the previous evening. Sunday morning provided time for party animals to recover from the weekend rituals. On arriving at church, I noticed that women usually outnumbered men by a significant margin. Then I thought about all of those talented young brothers asleep in the dorm.

Pondering the disconnection, I worried that the absence of tal-ented young men might hamper the black community's progress, leaving a shortage of leaders needed to serve with women in advancing the social and spiritual ministry of the community's most influential institution. This concern lingered as I pursued my education at Harvard Divinity School. In 1977, when the time came to declare a thesis project for the master's degree, I decided to give attention to this gender differential in church attendance.

My field study focused on the male exodus from the tradition-al black church. After conferring with professors and mentors Charles Willie of the School of Education and Preston Williams of

the Divinity School, I began to conduct group interviews and discussions at the Owens Barber Shop on Columbus Avenue in
Boston's South End. The idea of doing research in a barber shop
came from Dr. John Hope Franklin (no relation), who has
observed that beauty salons and barbershops provide ideal places
for tuning into a community's opinions. Mr. Owens and my barber,
Lee, kindly allowed me to hang around after my haircut in order to
raise questions with the patrons. I also convened a similar discussion group among Morehouse College graduates residing in the
Boston area, most of whom attended graduate and professional
schools. Since this group also met occasionally for support and fellowship, I was able to ask them more than once about their attendance at black churches and to record the responses.

The Exodus of Men

Institutional Factors

Among the reasons the college-educated men cited for not going to
church were: (1) the social-ethical teachings of Christianity encourage meekness and passivity, which are dysfunctional and dangerous qualities in street-corner culture; (2) the character traits of the
ideal Christian run counter to the macho persona; (3) most
churches seemed to turn away from risky social action after the civil
rights movement, expanding their internal operations instead; (4)
churches, even when involved in politics, are not sufficiently radical and prophetic, choosing to support rather than challenge the
political status quo (see the discussion in chapter 2 on varieties of
political activism); and (5) the sacred art, icons, and religious symbols of the church reflect European cultural values and ignore the
African presence in the Bible.

The men at the barbershop, in turn, gave the following reasons:
(1) worship services tend to be unnecessarily long, and leaders
seem to be indifferent toward time management; (2) churches are
too preoccupied with money and engage in heavy-handed fund-

raising that is often insensitive to poor people; and (3) churches seem to tolerate hypocrisy among important members and officers—the VIPs—but seek to induce guilt among ordinary members, especially with regard to personal morality (alcohol consumption, smoking, gambling, and sexual behavior).

Personal Factors

Each reason the respondents cited could be characterized as an institutional indictment. That is, the men found problems within the culture of the congregation or within the Christian tradition that were perceived as barriers to their participation. But the group from the barbershop named two additional factors, more personal and idiosyncratic, for their nonparticipation. First, some of the men noted that because of repeated moral failures they were not inclined to return to the church until they were truly ready to reform their lives. Second, some expressed general disinterest in organized religion and a preference for meeting spiritual needs in a more opportunistic, periodic, and eclectic ways. Some men said they belonged to fraternal orders through which they met their spiritual needs.

Hopeful Conclusions

I concluded in my thesis that both groups in the reasons they gave reflected much of the dissatisfaction with churches of the 1960s and early 1970s, which had yet to make adjustments in light of the civil rights revolution. Furthermore, I noted that (1) with the exception of one medical student, most of the men continued to believe in God and that their nonparticipation could not be interpreted as an embrace of atheism; (2) the men also continued to be affiliative and sought opportunities for group experience rather than detached individualism; and (3) most of the respondents were willing to consider visiting churches that had incorporated changes that responded to their concerns. This last conclusion I found particularly hopeful for congregations that could initiate innovations and thereby appeal to more people.

Return of the Exodus Men

Many have observed the return of men to black churches and, in growing numbers, to mosques, since the 1980s. While studying two Atlanta churches my Lilly-supported research team encountered evidence to support this observation. We saw in these congregations that men nearly equaled women in number; in both instances, the ministers had made the reclamation of men a cornerstone of their ministries.

Anecdotal evidence from around the nation seems to indicate that the congregations that have witnessed the greatest return of men have somehow incorporated the positive characteristics typical of black churches before the civil rights movement. (See chapter 2 for a fuller description of these characteristics.) Indeed, these congregations are doing well with all segments of the community, not just men. For this reason it might be more appropriate to speak of them as renewed black churches animated by a fresh vision of ministry and social theology. I shall say more about the characteristics of these churches in the final chapter.

> The congregations that have witnessed the greatest return of men have somehow incorporated the positive characteristics typical of black churches before the civil rights movement.

It should be noted, however, that the renewed congregations appeal to upwardly mobile, well-educated men with middle-class aspirations. The churches continue to be less attractive to men in the underclass who feel little loyalty to conventional economic structures, cultural values, family norms, and political and educational systems. This relatively small segment of the population will continue to challenge congregations and the rest of society to find ways to encourage their constructive participation. Failure to engage them will likely result in their long-term incarceration and/or high mortality rates.

Today in Atlanta the Antioch Baptist Church North is overrun by men, showing the changes that have occurred in the last decade. The pastor, Dr. Cameron Alexander, argues that the church must take more responsibility for rehearsing the African American journey from slavery to freedom for the current generation. "How else will they be integrated into the ongoing freedom struggle?" he asks. One Sunday in 1993 he invited men seated in the sanctuary to yield their seats to women who were standing, and to sit on the stairs surrounding the pulpit. The powerful image of men gathered around the altar registered. Dr. Alexander invited men to come to the stairs each week thereafter, and the practice continues. This illustration can serve as an object lesson for the pastor who regularly comments on the plight of black men, women, families, romance, and so forth, and who uses the occasion to teach listeners to be more responsible and caring in their interpersonal relations. Antioch Baptist Church North provides one compelling example of what can be done to attract men and to transform them from detached individualists into a community of care and accountability. Another encouraging sign of men seeking to make a greater impact on the moral direction of the society is their presence on the Mall in Washington on October 16, 1995.

Lessons from the Million Man March

Boarding a Delta Air Lines flight early that morning in Atlanta, I am embarrassed to admit that I was already worrying about what might be the lead sentence on the evening news. "Today, what was billed as a Million Man March proved to be a failure, attracting only a few thousand men." Or: "Tragic news from the nation's capital: an explosion set by a racist hate group killed scores of attendees at the Million Man March." Or: "Black men gathered in the name of peace and atonement ran for safety as gunfire between rival gangs caused rioting and chaos eventually quieted by the National Guard and police." I could imagine the grim faces of the anchors reading the awful news. I even envisioned ABC's *Nightline* program with its obligatory panel of experts (a gang leader, a black public intellectual, a law enforcement expert, and a civil rights leader) assembled to interpret the tragedy. Instead, the nation saw one of the largest gatherings ever in Washington, an extraordinary expression of personal and collective moral renewal by the nation's most enigmatic and often threatening portion of the population.

I traveled with Rev. Jonathan Greer, who was scheduled to speak on the crowded platform. Accompanying him enabled me to enter the Capitol building and to see the considerable security provided by police and Nation of Islam guards. I spent the next five or six hours standing next to the stage, watching a stream of celebrities. I could see Cornel West in the distance, waiting to be called to speak. Many of us who felt that he would offer a critique of anti-Semitism and black patriarchy in the Nation of Islam looked forward to his oration. But the oration never came. The master of ceremonies—and he was a master—continued to "place" celebrities behind the microphone while moving some of the more scholarly, independent thinkers farther back.

> *The Million Man March was an extraordinary expression of personal and collective moral renewal by the nation's most enigmatic and often threatening portion of the population.*

Jesse Jackson was provocative while reminding us that, during slavery, the master forbade "big meetings." The Million Man March, he noted, was one of the biggest meetings ever to assemble in that place. Maya Angelou celebrated the dignity and peaceful demeanor of the throng. But one of the most extraordinary moments came when gang leaders from around the nation gathered on stage and began to apologize to the nation's mothers for the bloodshed they had sponsored. They urged gang members to observe an indefinite truce in turf wars. It was a phenomenal moment, but unfortunately almost none of the evening news programs showed it.

The other moment of truth and transcendence occurred when the emcee raised the offering, asking the crowd to lift their money into the air while repeating the words, "This dollar will never be used to buy dope, or a gun, or a sister's body." Suddenly this simple gesture had changed the meaning of a dollar; money had become an instrument of moral expression.

Before the end of the day I ended up in a small circle on stage in which Jesse Jackson, Jr., was inviting rappers such as Ice-T and Ice-Cube to assist him in his bid for a Chicago congressional seat. Nearby I saw singer Isaac Hayes, filmmaker John Singleton, actor Will Smith, athlete Jim Brown, and public intellectual Michael Dyson, who informed me that he, too, was scheduled to speak for three minutes, but that so were seventy-one others. The day was growing short. People clearly were ready for Farrakhan's grand entrance, which followed moments later.

I will not comment on his speech except to say that the subject was inspired, even if the speech itself was disappointing and ponderous. He announced that he would speak about "A More Perfect Union." Thirty minutes into the oration I could see people beginning to detach from the messenger. Though his window of engagement was closing slowly, he seemed not to apprehend it. As I inched off the stage and into the crowd, headed for the subway station, I saw thousands of others making a reverse pilgrimage home, satisfied that they had at some level atoned, that they had showed up for an altar call, that they had been prayed for several times and challenged by eloquent women and children. They had heard songs of joy, triumph, and encouragement, and had contributed money to express support for this moral crusade. At the end of the day they did not need the long sermon that seemed tacked on to an otherwise coherent and meaningful liturgical movement. As the social critic and journalist Stanley Crouch later observed, Farrakhan had the greatest opportunity of any black leader in history to address the nation, and he blew it.

I drew the following lessons from the event. First, men from various backgrounds can assemble for religious and politically constructive purposes. Many fellow marchers noted how extraordinary it was to see so many come to an event not centered around sports or entertainment.

Second, Christians and Muslims can collaborate in seeking to revitalize troubled communities. Rev. Benjamin Chavis, former executive director of the NAACP, has highlighted this point by converting and joining the Nation of Islam, and by trying to show that different religious communities in black America can cooperate peacefully.

Third, meetings limited to one gender may not be the best way of constructing male–female partnerships aimed at gender reconciliation and community development. This has been a contested point in community discourse after the march. Many black women, like my wife, who insisted that I attend, believe that it was important and a sign of hope for men to gather and to transact business, sacred and mundane, without women. They supported the presence of the men in their lives at roll call. Other black women, however, were suspicious and critical of this effort to segregate the community by gender, particularly when the patriarchal Nation of Islam seemed to be sponsoring the crusade for renewal. It remains to be seen whether such gender-exclusive meetings help or hurt the general state of relations between black men and women.

Fourth, leaders on the fringe of the community who try to undertake worthy projects do not possess the authority or influence necessary to mobilize and sustain broad community participation. Louis Farrakhan and Benjamin Chavis Muhammad do not command broad or deep support in most black communities. By virtue of their charisma, daring, and organizational prowess, however, they fill a vacuum left by conventional leaders. For this reason, mainstream voices such as Cornel West have worked hard to engage, challenge, and rehabilitate Farrakhan within the court of public opinion.

Youth Programs That Work

In a discussion of effective youth development programs, educator Benjamin Canada has noted that "mentoring, monitoring, and ministering" have the greatest impact. *Mentoring* refers to a relationship of care and supervision that a responsible adult can have with a younger person. Most mentoring programs, including the vast majority of church-sponsored programs, are volunteer-based.

Observers note that because volunteers tend to spend only a few hours per week with their protégés, they are limited in their influence. The next wave of mentoring programs will place a responsible, caring adult in the life of every young person who desires a mentor. These mentors will be paid staff. The most extensive program has been developed by the Corporation for National Service, initiated by President Clinton, and the National Urban League in New York. Churches should decide on the nature and extent of mentoring that they can initiate and sustain. It would be exciting to see several churches join forces to support a mentor or two for the young men in their communities.

Monitoring refers to the careful tracking of the academic or job performance of young people and calling attention to trends. The Urban Institute noted that in 1986, 57 percent of black boys between 10 and 14 were two or more years behind their grade level at school.[8] Poor academic performance is the single most important predictor for children dropping out of school and for later unemployment or employment at low wages, and school officials see the warning signs before most others in the community.

Churches should work to design and implement programs that contribute to the character development of young people.

Many churches sponsor after-school programs of educational enrichment focusing on specific skill areas. For instance, the American Association for the Advancement of Science has sponsored a math and science program in more than three hundred black congregations in twenty-five cities. Churches can play a more active role in monitoring the educational progress of all of the young people in the community.

Another significant dimension in monitoring is the community's responsibility to support young offenders who seek to stay out of the criminal justice system. Churches could help create a matrix of police, school, and nonprofit agencies to support young people in this aim. Churches should identify and support the training and

full-time employment of youth ministers to work with these institutions, and work to design and implement programs to contribute
to the character development of young people.

Ministering refers to the effort to teach values and self-love, and
to provide care and discipline from a religious perspective. Unlike
mentoring and monitoring, minister-
ing is a more sectarian enterprise which
should not be supported by public
funds. Ministering comprises part of
the mission of the church but should
not be considered a part of its public
policy agenda. Ministering encompass-
es all of the church's work in society,
works of charity, mercy, peacemaking,
and justice-seeking. Ministry is the
church's response to the extravagant love and grace of God.

> *Ministering encompasses all of the church's work in society, works of charity, mercy, peacemaking, and justice-seeking. Ministry is the church's response to the extravagant love and grace of God.*

In April 1997 President Clinton, along with former Presidents
Gerald Ford, Jimmy Carter, and George Bush, collaborated in host-
ing a Presidents' Summit on the future of America. Led by General
Colin Powell, thousands of community leaders and business representatives explored ways of reviving civil society through volunteerism. Each of the strategies mentioned above was prominent in
the discussion. Despite the lip service paid to the role of religious
communities in restoring civil society, many participants with religious affiliations felt that communities of faith were not taken seriously and are not central to the project.

Such controversies aside, many commentators agree that communities have the knowledge at present to deal with problems confronting youth. In a 1988 publication titled "Within Our Reach,"
Lisbeth Schorr remarked that "we know how to intervene to reduce
the rotten outcomes of adolescence and to help break the cycle that
reaches into succeeding generations." In *Adolescence at Risk*, Joy
Dryfoos concluded that "enough is known about the lives of disadvantaged high-risk youth to mount an intensive campaign to alter
the trajectories of these children."[9]

According to research by the Eisenhower Foundation, the following actions have proven effective: (1) preschool programs, with the observation that every dollar spent on Head Start has resulted in $4.75 of benefits; (2) greater roles for parents and teachers in managing schools; (3) after-school programs like Big Brothers and Big Sisters; (4) the creation of "safe havens" during after-school hours, as advocated by the Children's Defense Fund; (5) increased community policing; (6) added resources for job training and placement; and (7) neighborhood development projects, such as those undertaken by community development corporations.

Several private foundations have launched national programs to benefit young black males and, indirectly, all stakeholders in the community. The Ford Foundation has supported a Fatherhood Initiative which aids programs that promote paternal responsibility and involvement. The funding initiative is directed by Dr. Ronald Mincy, an expert on the behavior of black urban males. Similarly, sociologist and philanthropist Dr. Bobby Austin of the William Klark Kellogg Foundation has sponsored an African American Male Initiative to support community projects operating in fifteen U.S. cities.

Despite the challenges young black males face, the good news is that they can be redeemed, as can all young people who have gone the way of the biblical prodigal son. The broad awareness of the tribulations and temptations confronting urban males has generated exciting programs throughout the church and society. We must pray, work, and hope that individuals and institutions will be moved to address the problems of youth systematically and coherently, coordinating the interventions of various sectors of the community. It is a sign of hope that these men have shown a capacity to act as moral agents, not passive victims, able to admit their need for atonement and reconciliation, and to take practical and unconventional steps to effect change.

> We must pray, work, and hope that individuals and institutions will be moved to address the problems of youth systematically and coherently, coordinating the interventions of various sectors of the community.

Despite the many negative portraits of young black and brown youths in our society, there are vast numbers living productive, positive lives. They deserve generous support from every sector of society. On behalf of those who have had trouble moving forward, churches, youth development experts, juvenile justice officials, school authorities, and other concerned stakeholders in the community should act now to cooperate in the support of these young people. All those who desire a second chance, who want to do the right thing, should find an open door and a helping hand. In the next chapter I will describe how churches and faith-based institutions can approach foundations and other entities for financial and technical support of their community development activities.

5 RESOURCES FOR THE LONG HAUL

After more than nine years as a seminary professor, I felt restless and in need of new intellectual stimulation and new opportunities to serve. Thanks to a nomination from Lawrence Jones, former dean of the School of Divinity at Howard University, my name and professional interests came to the attention of the Ford Foundation, which was searching for someone familiar with African American churches. In September 1994 I joined the foundation as a consultant and four months later became a program officer for the human rights and social justice section, led by a remarkable lawyer and philanthropist, Lynn Walker Huntley. Most of my friends regarded it as an odd career move, but in retrospect it was an invaluable stop along the journey to becoming a public theologian.

Religion and Foundations

Far from feeling suppressed or discouraged to talk about religion, most foundation staff were anxious to learn all they could about an increasingly potent sector of American public life to which they had not previously been attentive. In addition, both of the foundation's presidents with whom I had the pleasure of working, Franklin A. Thomas and Susan V. Berresford, were thoughtful, open-minded, and friendly toward the religious community and its potential for contributing to human betterment.

In addition to numerous lunchtime discussions with staff from every sector of the foundation, I had many opportunities to share my ideas about religion as a social force. One of my favorite venues was electronic-mail discussions, which included staff from the international field offices. I was somewhat surprised to discover that most of my literate and sophisticated colleagues' knowledge of religion in the modern world stopped with secularization theory, that is, the notion that since the European Enlightenment and the rise of scientific reasoning, religion and faith were no longer meaningful modes of interpreting reality. They were familiar and comfortable with the critiques of religion offered by Freud, Marx, and Darwin, but generally unaware of liberation theology, process theology, and other innovative forms of religious thought that incorporate the insights of contemporary social science, using them to renew theological reflection on the human condition. These discussions culminated in an extraordinary international staff meeting in Cairo during the month of Ramadan. The foundation is still in the process of more clearly defining its interests in the role of religion in the contemporary world.

Much younger than the well-known foundations established by John D. Rockefeller and Andrew Carnegie, the Ford Foundation was established in 1936 and now considers itself a resource for innovative individuals and institutions worldwide. Through its supply of grants, for many years it has attempted to increase participation in society by historically disadvantaged and vulnerable groups such as ethnic minorities, women, refugees, and immigrants. In an effort to focus resources more effectively in African American communities, the foundation decided to explore working with and through the most abundant, historic, and resourceful institutions in the black community, its churches and clergy.

In 1983 the Ford Foundation established an initiative to improve African American churches' ability to deliver secular social services. The initiative included four types of grants. First, the foundation provided support for research and documentation of the community service activities of black churches. As an organization guided by fresh data and new knowledge, the foundation believed that it was critical to demonstrate that churches were already serving the public good, not merely sectarian interests. Research would point to possible fields of collaboration between philanthropy and religion, and would highlight gaps in service delivery which churches and other nonprofit organizations might address.

> The Ford Foundation believed that it was critical to demonstrate that churches were already serving the public good, not merely sectarian interests.

Second, the Foundation invested in leadership development programs, guided by the research of sociologists Andrew Billingsley and C. Eric Lincoln, who suggested that one of the most reliable predictors of whether a church would undertake community service ministries was the education, experience, and outlook of the senior minister. Experts on the black church speculated that less than 20 percent of black clergy had received formal theological education. Furthermore, those enrolled in graduate seminaries received almost no training in program development, strategic planning, fund-raising, program administration, or public relations. Hence it seemed appropriate to find ways of supplementing the graduate theological curriculum. This was done by providing one-year fellowships to seminarians for placement in secular organizations such as community development corporations, youth development agencies, and public health institutions. In such settings they would be immersed in the culture of organizations from which they could learn valuable and transferable skills. Support was also provided to expand the work of the Institute on Church Administration and Management at the Interdenominational Theological Center in Atlanta. With initial funding from the Lilly Endowment, the institute provides training in program development and management to seminarians as well as current pastors and laypersons interested in expanding their public ministries.

Third, the foundation supported regional and national organizations for training and technical assistance in community economic development, after-school math and science programs, teen pregnancy prevention, and so forth. The foundation sought to build a national infrastructure for nonprofit groups that might require assistance with technical, financial, legal, and management issues, or funds for implementing new programs. National donors such as the Ford Foundation have developed effective partnerships with community and regional foundations that share an appreciation for public-spirited faith communities.

Fourth, in an effort to increase the number of donors that share in the foundation's vision, support has been provided for education and outreach efforts within the philanthropic community. Through annual national conferences, regional meetings between church leaders and philanthropists, publications, and videotapes the number of foundation and faith-community partnerships is on the rise.

Notable among foundations which have backed faith groups in their community service activities is the Lilly Endowment (Indianapolis), which has probably provided more support for black church programs than any other funding entity. The Pew Charitable Trusts (Philadelphia) has supported a variety of programs sponsored by religious organizations and currently has a special interest in Latino religious communities. The William Klark Kellogg Foundation (Battle Creek, Michigan) has supported church-sponsored programs to enhance health services and the development of young men. The Carnegie Corporation and the DeWitt Wallace-Readers Digest Foundation (New York) have supported programs aimed at children and youth development. And foundation executives at the Rockefeller Foundation (New York) and the Annie E. Casey Foundation (Baltimore) have been in dialogue with religious leaders about possible areas of collaboration, including the state of race relations in America.

There has been a good deal of experimentation in regional and community foundations with both systematic and periodic support for projects in faith communities. For instance, in Boston the Hyams Foundation has helped a nonprofit community development ministry known as the Ten-Point Coalition, which provides comprehensive services for youth. The Piton Foundation in Denver has established the Metro-Denver Black Church Initiative. In Jackson, Mississippi, the Foundation for the Mid-South has established an African American Church and Community Development Project to provide training, technical support, and mini-grants to faith-based organizations in Mississippi, Arkansas, and Louisiana. Fortunately, momentum continues to build throughout the nation as each year new projects are being developed.

Five Levels of Faith-Based Community Activity

Currently, the faith community is engaged in at least five levels of service to the larger community. First, congregations engage in *basic charity* when they provide immediate, direct relief to the hungry, homeless, those needing medical care, and so on. The second level of service is *sustained support* to help people become self-reliant and capable of securing and holding employment. Independent Sector, a private research agency in Washington, found that in 1992 nine out of ten congregations provided charity in the area of human services and health, and six out of ten provided some "public, societal benefit."[1] The third level is *social service delivery*, which involves a long-term institutional commitment to providing services such as child and elder care, literacy skills, and job training and placement to local residents and to others who can afford it. Government agencies, which otherwise would have to provide the services themselves, often subsidize these efforts. It saves money when the public sector contracts with private agencies, including faith-based institutions, to provide services thought essential to a life of dignity. Currently, one-third of child care services in the United States are provided by faith-based institutions; Catholic Charities USA and Lutheran Social Services in America rely on the government for 60 percent of their operating expenses.[2]

> It saves money when the public sector contracts with private agencies, including faith-based institutions, to provide services thought essential to a life of dignity.

The fourth level is *political advocacy*, which involves a congregation or coalition of faith communities in representing the needs of the least advantaged in society before government entities that have budget responsibilities, and before the media, which portrays the lives of these citizens. Among the most effective examples of this type of service are the U.S. Council of Catholic Bishops, the National Council of Churches of Christ, which maintains a Washington legislative office, and the Congress of National Black Churches in Washington.

The fifth and most ambitious level of intervention is *comprehensive community development*. At this level churches take the lead or serve as partners in the comprehensive revitalization and development of a community, taking care of housing needs, assisting in the birth and growth of microenterprises, strengthening small businesses, sponsoring large retail and franchise entities, acquiring and providing credit and venture capital, and engaging in other enterprises to encourage job creation and self-sufficiency. Exciting examples of this model abound, including the East Brooklyn Council of Churches, which has backed the Nehemiah Project in its construction of more than thirty thousand attractive, affordable housing units for low-income people. In Los Angeles the First African Methodist Episcopal Church, with assistance from the Walt Disney Corporation, has initiated a comprehensive program to rebuild neighborhoods destroyed during the Los Angeles uprisings of 1992. In Philadelphia, Rev. Leon Sullivan served as an early proponent of church-sponsored community development when he helped build a multimillion-dollar retail shopping complex known as Liberty Plaza. In nearly every major urban center in the country, one can identify exciting projects sponsored by communities of faith.

At this time of increased government and public interest in empowering faith-based organizations for community revitalization and social service delivery—activities that require significant capital and technical support—I would urge all faith communities to consider how they might expand their current level of community service. Churches working at lower levels of engagement should decide how they can move up the scale of social ministry.

The Prophetic Imperative

The religious community and, in my view, Christians especially, bring important values to community development, including: (1) a commitment to serving the poor and other less advantaged members of humanity; (2) a keen sense of respect for nature and the impact of development on our fragile ecology; (3) a deep sense of stewardship over resources, encouraging greater attention to balance between human need and material goods; (4) a sense of vocation or calling to their work, manifesting itself in a drive for success and competence, a subject of interest from Luther to Max Weber; (5) a desire to practice honesty and cooperation, valuable assets to have in the workplace.

But churches bring something else to the development enterprise, what I would call the prophetic perspective and imperative. As churches contribute to the development of neighborhood economies, they should recall their mission of *prophetic* witness, of raising critical questions about the moral and social effects of market economics. This constitutes part of Martin Luther King's unfinished agenda. Perhaps Mahatma Gandhi best expressed the prophetic spirit of religion when he described the seven deadly sins as "politics without principle, wealth without work, commerce without morality, pleasure without conscience, education without character, science without humanity, and worship without sacrifice."[3]

In this spirit the church must ask, "What impact is development having on the dignity of individuals, the stability of families,
the health of local residents and the natural surroundings, the
quality of civic life, and the overall fulfillment of people?" Given its
special identity and mission, the church should attempt to sustain
a creative tension between its roles in community development
and as a prophetic moral agent. Our mastery of the art of making
money and empowering communities economically must never let
us lose sight of our distinctive mission in the world.

But how will churches nurture this creative tension and how
will they remember their distinctive perspective on the development game? How can we renew our biblical, theological, and ethical commitments and our identities as believers? The answer is
simple: through vibrant, earnest wor-
ship. It is in worship that churches are
called to remember that One to whom
we are accountable, and through
whom we have been liberated to love
and serve boldly. In worship we can
revisit the central narrative of God's
love for humanity and our inclination
to selfishness and sin. In worship, we
collide with the core values of the reli-
gious tradition that gives us new names, new responsibilities, and
new rewards. In worship we are called to the altar, where we can
repent for our sins in the marketplace and find grace to reenter the
fray. *Good worship is essential for prophetic, faith-based community
development.*

> *Given its special identity and
> mission, the church should attempt
> to sustain a creative tension
> between its roles in community
> development and as a
> prophetic moral agent.*

This call represents a challenge and invitation to those who are
not members of a faith community. Our fellow citizens should try
to answer such questions as, "Where and how are your identities,
values, and vision critically examined, renewed, forgiven, and reen-
ergized? As many of us learned from the civil rights movement, rituals of personal and spiritual renewal are essential to keeping a
passion for justice focused and vibrant. Our focus on social trans-

formation must relate to personal transformations, a topic that I addressed in an previous book, *Liberating Visions: Human Fulfillment and Social Justice in African American Thought* (Fortress, 1990).

Lessons from Foundation–Church Partnerships

During my years in philanthropy, I had numerous opportunities to meet with donors and church leaders seeking to develop mutually empowering partnerships. In work with colleagues such as Lynn Huntley (Southern Education Foundation), Emmett Carson (Minneapolis Foundation), Dean Lawrence Jones (Howard University Divinity School), Rev. Audrey Daniel (Council on Foundations), and Jacqui Burton (The College Fund), we visited gatherings of community workers throughout the nation. Although it would be impossible to distill all of the valuable lessons that emerged from those conversations, I will attempt to summarize the major lessons.

The System Is the Relationship

First, the cultures of philanthropy and the African American church, generally speaking, are quite different. Although both are defined by certain norms, guided by particular values, and judged according to shared standards of professional practice, their inner dynamics diverge radically. Organized philanthropy shares much of the formal, bureaucratic culture of corporations and government agencies. By contrast, churches are voluntary associations that place value on nurturing informal, kinship-like relationships. Such relationships foster trust, facilitate mutual caring and support, and may empower people to work on behalf of the common good.

For churches, the relationship is the system. Through relation ships, the work of the church is accomplished. Churches do not need to become bureaucratic to fulfill their mission. Their style of record-keeping, for instance, tends to be somewhat idiosyncratic and more relaxed than would be expected in a social service agency. The important thing is that someone knows the state of financial and organizational health in the congregation. When that is not the case, congregations need to seek assistance in organizing internal operations to make themselves better stewards of the community's resources and to be eligible for outside revenue to help serve the community. Churches don't have to be businesses, but they do have to be more business-like in accounting for their accomplishments.

Churches must understand that donors need accurate, timely records and reports of how funds are being used and what activities are being pursued. Donors, on the other hand, must appreciate the challenge of trying to maintain effective service-delivery programs and efficient office operations on a shoestring budget and with inadequate staffing. Donors should permit larger percentages of grant money to support the general operations of faith-based projects. And churches must be exceedingly careful not to mingle donor funds with church funds.

> *Churches don't have to be businesses, but they do have to be more business-like in accounting for their accomplishments.*

Donors understand that quality relationships are central to negotiating grants. Therefore, they must trust the capacity of leaders and church workers to accomplish their stated objectives. Since both sectors appreciate the importance of relationship building, it would be useful for them to begin conversations about their perspectives on social problems as well as their missions, goals, and strategies for promoting human fulfillment. Church leaders and donors should now be practicing the art of fellowship.

One Reality Can Have Many Names

Given the contrasting work cultures of churches and foundations, both possess different languages or idioms for describing their work. This has often been a source of confusion and frustration for donors and grant seekers. As a grant maker, every week I received proposals that referred to the congregation's efforts to serve the Lord and to save humanity. Ordinarily, such language would not take that proposal very far in a secular foundation. On a few occasions I called the clergyperson to inquire about the activities in which the church was engaged. Without prompting, she or he would describe a host of social service activities the church sponsored, probably with greater impact than the government counterparts. Social service activities were eligible for funding; most clergy understood that the foundation would not provide support for evangelism and proselytizing.

Lynette Campbell, an executive with the Philadelphia Foundation, notes that while churches often talk about mission, foundations are more comfortable speaking of service-delivery activities and objectives. She observes that both groups need to learn to translate the other's distinctive vocabulary.

Proactive Donors Catalyze Partnerships

For most Americans, the world of philanthropy is shrouded in mystery; to most churchgoers it is invisible. Even Dorothy Riddings, the president of the Council on Foundations, says that philanthropists must do a better job informing the public of their good work. Most church leaders and workers who are immersed in community development and social service do not have time to explore the esoteric field of philanthropy. These leaders ask that donors work proactively to educate faith-driven community servants about possibilities for training, technical support, expansion, seed grants, coalition-building with other service agencies, and assistance in self-evaluation. Donors can also help potential grant seekers understand what the foundation expects in terms of written reports, financial records, timelines of projected activity, and evidence of adequate governance over the project.

Donors working with faith communities could also help other foundations with advice about funding church-based projects. Often, donors need to be assured that there are no legal or tax prohibitions in making grants to religious organizations. Fortunately, the Council on Foundations has published information that addresses these concerns. Providing counsel to colleagues in philanthropy interested in innovative partnerships became a significant task for staff at the Ford Foundation.

Churches Practice Philanthropy as Well

The field of philanthropy has its roots in the great religious traditions of the world. Churches, synagogues, temples, mosques, and other communities of faith have long practiced charity, local empowerment, and social change. It is important for donors to realize that churches already use their financial and human assets to promote human betterment. In many instances, churches themselves make grants to other institutions and individuals. For instance, Brooklyn's Concord Baptist Church, using funds from a small endowment, makes small grants each year to community-based organizations such as bookstores, cultural centers, mentoring programs, and so on. Increasingly, churches seek regard as equal partners in the donor–church equation, rather than being perceived solely as institutions that ask for money. With the rise of so many affluent congregations in the African American community, and with the significant transfer of wealth from older generations projected in the next decade, I would hope that the movement to endow churches and to develop church-based philanthropy accelerates dramatically.

Sometimes Money Hurts More than It Helps

Many local church leaders report that the infusion of large sums of foundation money into a bare-bones operation can actually hurt, fostering dependency and exposing personal and institutional rivalries not evident before. Dolphus Weary, executive director of Mendenhall Ministries in the Mississippi delta, observes that people can feel disempowered when new funds arrive. Sometimes they no longer feel responsible for supporting community service programs themselves. This echoes the concern many have with regard to the unintended negative effects of welfare payments.

This illustration may serve as an important lesson for both donors and church leaders as they structure what churches need to serve and develop communities more effectively. As George Penick of the Foundation for the Mid-South notes, church leaders often approach the foundation seeking advice and technical assistance for organizing and implementing new programs. The foundation must listen carefully and try to identify the optimal combination of technical assistance and program money. One of the truisms of human history is that money changes things. Steven Tipton of Emory University used to jokingly remind me of the many new friends I had acquired after joining the foundation, noting that money is a force field that pulls on everything. In several instances, fragile coalitions in churches have fractured due to the prospect of attaining foundation money. Some of my most agonizing visits to church leaders involved the tough decision not to recommend a grant because it would compromise the very coalition that we were seeking to promote.

Following this truncated list of lessons from my experience with church–donor dialogue, I offer below some advice to church- and other community-based leaders on how to seek grants.

What to Remember When Seeking Foundation Support

Before approaching a foundation, do your homework. Research the foundation's interests, history, and current funding priorities. If the foundation focuses primarily on one or two areas, submitting a proposal for a project in an unrelated field will be a waste of time.

Get to know someone at the foundation, or at least find out to whom you might correspond. Letters not addressed to an individual are generally not treated as seriously as other letters. Contact friends in the business or nonprofit communities who might know someone at the foundation and who might assist your approach.

Send a letter of inquiry (LOI) before sending a proposal. The content of the letter will vary according to the donor's requirements, with which you should be acquainted. The LOI should do three things: (*a*) introduce your church and staff to the foundation; (*b*) say what you would like to do with their support; and (*c*) ask for the name of a person to whom you should send the proposal, and for any other information that the foundation will need. Indicate that you would like to submit a full proposal and will follow up with a call a week after sending the letter. It helps if the foundation asks you to submit a full proposal.

The proposal is an institutional resumé. Make sure that it presents your church accurately and positively. The basic elements of a proposal include (*a*) a brief paragraph specifying who you are, what you propose to do, and how much money you seek and over what period of time; (*b*) a background description of the problem you seek to address; (*c*) a description of the activities you propose to undertake; (*d*) a timeline indicating when you intend to implement each activity; (*e*) a budget for the project; (*f*) the qualifications of those who will do the work; (*g*) a list of governing board and advisers; (*h*) proof of tax-exempt status; and (*i*) an outline of your plan for evaluations at the midway point and at the end of the grant term. Carefully prepare these documents and make sure that they are proofread by at least two meticulous people. Type the proposal in an easy-to-read format; highlight the major topics or themes so that the most important points stand out when eyes scan the page. Send at least two copies of the proposal. Often the original is routed through the foundation's mail system, which can delay a program officer in giving immediate attention to your material.

Invite the program officer for a site visit or offer to meet the program officer at the foundation. Remember that you are building a relationship and that people tend to give money to other people, not to programs. When officers visit, don't overdo the hospitality. It tends to make them self-conscious and embarrassed. On one visit to an organization in a small Midwestern city, I discovered a huge neon sign welcoming me (and the foundation, of course) to town. It was nice for my ego, but it didn't help them get the grant. In fact, it left me concerned about their frivolous use of money. And, by all means, do not do anything that might be construed as unethical. A tiny number of grant seekers are so desperate for foundation money that they cross the line of propriety by offering bribes or other inappropriate services.

If the foundation cannot respond favorably, ask for advice about other places to submit the proposal. Don't walk away content with a negative response. View the foundation executive as a technical assistant who knows more than you do about the world of philanthropy. Try to pick her brain for ideas about your fundraising strategy. I know that my foundation friends will cringe at that suggestion. But Franklin Thomas, the former president of the Ford Foundation, used to remind the staff regularly that we were public servants practicing philanthropy with the blessing of public consent. Still, do not become a pest to foundation staff. Remember that they are very busy people who may wish to assist you but may not have the time. Ask for help, but leave it at that.

I would be cautious about arranging a call from a VIP to the head of a foundation in order to expedite a proposal. Foundation presidents tend to trust the judgment of their program staff who have worked on the proposal directly. Attempting to use an influential friend to advance a grant request may be perceived as compensation for the lack of a quality proposal. One other caution about such power plays: once you've spent that currency, you can't use it again at that foundation.

Assessing Programs and Proposals

With these suggestions in mind, I now offer a list of prominent ideas and terms in the foundation world. First and foremost is *capacity*. This is the demonstrable ability to accomplish your mission in an effective, efficient manner. Does your church or agency accomplish tasks professionally, reliably, and predictably? Do you have a plan to ensure that all of your employees receive the continuing education necessary to fulfill their responsibilities? Do you have a plan to have your work evaluated by an outside consultant? Does your organization learn from its work and communicate these lessons to others inside the organization and to the public? A church that does not have a sense of its capacity should consider approaching donors about capacity-building funds. A capacity-building grant would enable the project staff to receive the necessary training for the proposed activities. Foundations tend to be

more comfortable providing capacity-building grants before providing project funds.

Second, foundations look for *innovation*. My favorite definition
of innovation comes from Booker T. Washington, who spoke of the
virtue of doing common things in an uncommon manner. Innovation is one way of speaking about creative ability, and foundations
are custodians of the culture's creativity. Innovation manifests itself
in a variety of ways; for instance, in the way a problem is framed.
Rather than seeing the presence of youth gangs as a desire for violence, gang affiliation could also be viewed as youthful hunger for
community, structure, membership, trust, loyalty, and commitment.
Programs that reframe the gang problem by focusing on the vacuum
that gangs fill, and that seek to redirect those energies more positively, bring a missing ingredient to the debate about youth development. Innovation is also manifested in project design and out-
come. For instance, the Grameen Bank of Bangladesh started its
community development efforts with a very small loan to rural
women, who agreed to repay the money into a revolving fund. The
bank now serves hundreds of thousands of people with modest
incomes who are working toward self-sufficiency. Those whom conventional lenders regarded as bad credit risks have proven to be
good economic stewards, with one of the lowest default rates of any
credit program.

Third, donors seek to invest in organizations that engage in *collaboration*. Former Surgeon General Jocelyn Elders defined collaboration as an unnatural act between two nonconsenting adults. The
humor in her comment underscores the difficulty of getting organizations and individuals to work on a common task. Since money
from donors is modest in relation to money in the corporate or
government arenas, donors are compelled to be strategic when
making grants, always seeking the greatest impact for a limited
amount of funds. Churches that cooperate in delivering services or
in developing the community are more likely to receive funding
than other groups. Often, national donors like Ford and Lilly limit
their support to regional or national coalitions such as the Con-

gress of National Black Churches in Washington, which has produced one of the better manuals on coalition building among religious institutions. I should add that donors are impressed when unlikely partners collaborate for the common good. For instance, when a coalition is not only ecumenical, but also interfaith, interracial, or international, it possesses a dimension that is too rarely seen, and may generate excitement among donors.

Fourth, many donors look to promote *local empowerment* by supporting proposals that will have an impact on those most affected by social problems. This approach seeks to increase the decision-making capacities and other resources of neighborhood residents, rather than increasing the capacity of the professional organizations that serve them. The Catholic principle of the subsidiary captures this idea by proposing that ministry should lessen the influence of government and market on family and neighborhood life.

Fifth, donors are more likely to support projects that can demonstrate *sustainability*. The leaders of faith-based projects would serve their interests if they were to consider and indicate how the project will continue beyond the time of the grant. They should be able to show the extent of their financial commitment, the names of other committed or prospective donors, and the amount of in-kind contributions. They should also anticipate how the project could be downsized without being terminated.

Sixth, most donors are concerned about *evaluation*. They want to ensure that a disinterested, relatively objective consultant will be able to verify a project's effectiveness. Foundations often require an evaluation by an outside source before renewing a grant. Hence leaders should develop an evaluation plan at the outset. This planning also conveys confidence in the quality of the project and the integrity of its staff.

Finally, donors concerned about the deterioration of civil society and volunteerism in America are anxious to see how a proposed project will promote what could be called, in a word, *civility*. Those who track declining rates of voter participation worry about the changing notions of citizenship. Many people feel entitled to goods and rights, but do not consider their responsibility for strengthening democracy. The future of American democracy depends in large measure on the stake that the great, silent majority has in society. Projects that promote, in some manner, the arts of good citizenship, such as voting, running for office, volunteer service, public debate, courteousness, compassion, hard work, and a kind disposition, will earn the attention of donors concerned about these matters. These aims relate to innovation as well. Projects focused on job creation, child care, or violence prevention can also be organized to inculcate or to reinforce civic virtues. Such considerations would add value to a project that does not focus explicitly on building character for a civil society.

> *Projects that promote the arts of good citizenship will earn the attention of donors concened about these matters.*

Although there is no surefire way to attain funds, I hope that these tips will help grant seekers carefully examine their projects, proposals, and overall fund-raising strategies prior to approaching donors. I close with my favorite quotation by W. E. B. Du Bois, who had much to say about the virtue of civic responsibility manifested in personal service and sacrifice. Speaking at a commencement ceremony at Howard University in 1939, Du Bois said:

> When I say sacrifice, I mean sacrifice. I mean a real and definite surrender of personal ease and satisfaction. . . . To increase abiding satisfaction for the mass of our people, and for all people, someone must sacrifice something of his own happiness. This is a duty only to those who recognize it as a duty. It is silly to tell intelligent human beings: Be good and you will be happy. The truth is today, be good, be decent, be honorable and self-sacrificing and you will not always be happy. You will often be desperately unhappy. You may even be crucified, dead, and buried, and the third day you will be just as dead as the first. But, with the death of your happiness, may easily come increased happiness, and satisfaction, and fulfillment for other people—strangers, unborn babes, uncreated worlds. If this is not sufficient incentive, never try it—remain hogs.[4]

6 VISION FOR THE JOURNEY

In 1996, the film *Jerry Maguire* was nominated for an Academy Award for best picture. The film starred Tom Cruise, a handsome, popular Hollywood star who in the title role played a sports agent in the midst of an emotional breakdown. Jerry Maguire, locked in his apartment, turns on his laptop computer in an effort to seek relief and redemption. He sets out to write a one-paragraph mission statement for his life, hoping that it will serve as a compass for the journey ahead. When he stops writing he has a twenty-five-page statement, outlining the necessity of instituting more humane practices and values into the corporate culture. He feels relieved after sending a copy to all of his colleagues, but is soon fired for pushing against the corporate grain. He finds spiritual fulfillment in a simpler life marked by honesty, commitment, sacrifice, and service. When a Hollywood superstar like Tom Cruise has a spiritual crisis on the big screen and touches millions of viewers, something significant is happening in our culture.

Clearly, large numbers of people are on a journey to discover spiritual fulfillment. The Gallup Poll organization continues to report that more than 90 percent of Americans believe in God. National news magazines regularly feature cover stories on prayer, angels, healing, the afterlife, and values. We have always known that America is a religious nation, marked by belief in God, church attendance, and appreciation for religious rituals such as weddings and so forth. But now it seems that Americans wish to become people with insight into the meaning of life and who commune with higher powers.

For people seeking to satisfy their spiritual search in organized religion, I think that a special kind of leadership is needed. Before focusing on the qualities that leaders ought to cultivate, we should consider the challenge of leadership in a broader framework. Despite widespread cynicism concerning leadership in our society, we still can be moved by the presence of authentic moral guidance. In our time, President Nelson Mandela of South Africa, Cardinal Joseph Bernardin of Chicago, Mother Teresa, and former President Jimmy Carter have challenged us to suspend our cynicism and to support those striving to promote our highest values.

> *Despite widespread cynicism concerning leadership in our society, we still can be moved by the presence of authentic moral guidance.*

Perhaps the culture is waiting for more leaders of this sort. The problem is that they are not easily made. In fact, we don't know precisely what happens when a person becomes a leader. In his classic study of leadership, James MacGregor Burns has observed that

Leadership is a process of morality to the degree that leaders engage with followers on the basis of shared motives and values and goals. Leadership over human beings is exercised when persons with certain motives and purposes mobilize, in competition or conflict with others, institutional, political, psychological, and other resources so as to arouse, engage, and satisfy the motives of followers.

He also distinguishes two types of leadership. Transactional leadership establishes temporary contact with people for the purpose of exchanging valued things (jobs for votes, goods for money, or hospitality for a listening ear). Transformational leadership engages with others so that the leader and followers "raise one another to higher levels of motivation and morality." "Transforming leadership ultimately becomes moral in that it raises the level of human conduct and ethical aspiration of both leader and led, and thus it has a transforming effect on both. Perhaps the best modern example is Gandhi. . . . Transcending leadership is dynamic leadership in the sense that the leaders throw themselves into a relationship with followers who will feel 'elevated' by it and often become more active themselves, thereby creating new cadres of leaders."[1]

I would like to build on Burns's model of transformational leadership with a metaphor. Authentic leaders are like diamonds who typically exist in the rough, their value and potential unrecognized by most people. Over time a process of refinement occurs. The value within is hammered out through times of testing and crisis. Years of prison refined Mandela; a struggle with cancer gave Bernardin the power to teach us how to die with dignity; and a life devoted to serving the poor has transformed Mother Teresa into a saint who challenges the materialism of our time.

> *Authentic leaders are like diamonds who typically exist in the rough, their value and potential unrecognized by most people.*

Searching for Diamonds

I envision a diamond with seven facets, each representing a critical feature of religious leadership. I believe that all religious leaders and clergy should become public theologians like Martin Luther King, Benjamin E. Mays, Andrew Young, and Marian Wright Edelman of the Children's Defense Fund. Public theologians are committed to presenting their understandings of God along with their ethical principles and values to the public for scrutiny, discussion, and possible acceptance. In contrast to sectarian theologians who understand that they are speaking for and to the community of believers, public theologians understand themselves as ambassadors for Christ (2 Corinthians 5:20). They stand between worlds, representing the distinctive vision and virtues of Christianity to a secular culture. They stand in a particular faith tradition but seek to address people from all walks of life. And they do so with a deep respect for the belief systems that others may already hold. Consequently, public theologians move into the public arena with a profound sense of humility, reverence for the sacredness of people and traditions, and, in view of their manifold limitations, a sense of humor about their noble calling. This is part of what it means to be a fool for Christ. As fools, we know how and when to laugh at ourselves. How different religious conflicts would seem today if believers would pause to laugh at themselves, their conceits, their mistakes, and their aspirations, and that God has entrusted humans with such great treasures of grace and truth.

> *How different religious conflicts would seem today if believers would pause to laugh at themselves their conceits, their mistakes, and their aspirations, and that God has entrusted humans with such great treasures of grace and truth.*

The public theologian should first serve as an *anointed spiritual guide*. Spiritual guides understand their role in helping to lead people to a deeper experience of God. The spiritual guide, like a priest, mediates an encounter with the holy, sometimes through words, rituals, gestures, and silence. The guide also understands when to get out of the way.

Second, public theologians should be *grassroots intellectuals* who initiate and encourage informed public discussion. Such efforts revive the role of preachers in the early slave community, who often were the community's most literate members and were relied on as interpreters of reality. Ministers served as public intellectuals and educators. Although members of contemporary communities discuss issues in barber shops and beauty parlors, at social events, and on the street, these discussions often occur outside a governing moral framework or without a sense of how to translate dialogue into public action. Grassroots intellectuals can bring this dimension to the conversation.

Third, public theologians should be *civic enablers* who understand how to empower neighborhoods both through the political system and volunteerism. Civic enablers should ensure that community members take advantage of the benefits of citizenship through voting and by holding public officials accountable. As political power devolves to local communities, enablers should take responsibility for convening meetings with elected officials and insisting that these officials become educators, willing to give citizens the power to understand and affect discussions about public policy and spending. Enablers should also help people realize the power that can grow from organized activism.

Fourth, public theologians should be *stewards of community economic development*. They should recognize the potential economic power of billions of dollars in aggregate income that African Americans receive and organize ways to harness it for community development. As we discovered in the Hampton survey, 57 percent of clergy believe that churches should own for-profit businesses. Good stewards identify and seize opportunities to make financial resources work more effectively for the improvement of living conditions.

> Good stewards identify and seize opportunities to make financial resources work more effectively for the improvement of living conditions.

Fifth, leaders should be Afrocentric *cultural celebrants* who proudly affirm our African past and use it to enrich our personal and collective lives today. Celebrants should design rituals to teach values that animated traditional African societies. However, they must be critical celebrants who bring those values and practices into conformity with the core values of the African American Christian tradition. For instance, it would not be desirable to impose the patriarchal practices of some African societies on women and men in the American context, who are striving for respectful relationships. Celebrants should also seek to build bridges to non-Africans who wish to work together for a better society. As Dr. Manning Marable of Columbia University has noted, Afrocentric pluralism affirms particularity but also places its beliefs in relationship with the larger human family. By contrast, Afrocentric exclusivism seeks to separate humanity along racial and ethnic lines, thereby recapitulating the social evils which European racists had earlier accomplished.

Sixth, public theologians should be *family facilitators*. Recognizing the declining rates of marriage and family formation in the black community, they should promote a culture of marriage and family. They should design programs to address the needs of single people, married couples, single parents, and others. Ultimately, they should seek to facilitate the growth of extended family networks.

Finally, public theologians should be *technologically literate visionaries*, aware of emerging technologies and trying to harness their potential to improve lives. Rev. Martha Arinkatola, an ITC student, established a cyberspace church featuring music, homilies, prayers, and sacred art for Internet surfers desiring spiritual refreshment. Recall from *Jerry Maguire* that the computer can become a tool for self-discovery, renewal, and empowerment—a very different picture of technology from what we saw of the computer "Hal" in *2001: A Space Odyssey*.

Renewing American Society

My thesis is that the renewal of American civil society depends on vigorous religious groups doing their part to heal, reconcile, nurture, guide, discipline, and inspire individuals to join in authentic community. Churches can accomplish this goal in ways that differ from any other sector of civil society, incorporating the logic, as argued by Boston University economist Glenn Loury, that sustainable, good communities are built one person at a time, from the inside out.

My concern, however, is that African American churches are not as ready as they should be to meet the challenges ahead. Although all faith communities will have a role in the renewal of civil society, black churches play a unique role in black, underclass neighborhoods with few other community organizations. Since the symptoms of poverty are concentrated in these communities, the most promising solutions will emerge within their boundaries. However, churches and other change agents will need the assistance of outside partners and supporters to alleviate poverty in the long term.

The renewal of American civil society depends on vigorous religious groups doing their part to heal, reconcile, nurture, guide, discipline, and inspire individuals to join in authentic community.

During the 1997 commencement exercises at ITC, Dr. Gardner Taylor revisited the familiar passage from Ezekiel 37 regarding the valley of dry bones. He asked continually, "Can these bones live?" His question is suggestive for the challenges facing urban black churches. The renewal of inner-city black churches depends on a reckoning with the significant demographic, political, and cultural changes that have occurred in black communities since the civil rights movement. This process will involve self-assessment and self-criticism. Healing will come only after we admit our illness. The churches must ask the surrounding community for a report card on past stewardship efforts. Churches must ask residents how the church can be a better servant and partner in community development. Church leaders must accept the harsh criticisms and challenging suggestions, and even the outright rejection that some community members may express. This self-assessment will constitute part of the long and painful process of healing and empowerment that churches must undergo as they retool and re-engineer for the next century.

Churches and clergy must listen to indictments of their sinceri-ty, relevance, and commitment, not in a defensive posture, but with humility and humor to admit willingly that they have been part of the problem for too long. Congregations are often not taken seri-ously as change agents in the community because they appear to be on the sidelines, avoiding the messiness of community politics and power dynamics. During the process of renewal, congregations must explore how they can serve as voices for social righteousness with-out entangling themselves excessively in partisan politics or, at the other extreme, maintaining their noninvolvement. Recall Dante's admonition that the hottest places in hell are reserved for those who, in times of moral crisis, seek to maintain their neutrality.

The good news is that dry bones can live if they can stand tough medicine. Clergy should take hope from the numerous insti-tutions and resources available to assist in their retooling and lead-ership development. These include educational programs offered by the Institute on Church Administration and Management at ITC, the Congress of National Black Churches, the Urban Min-istries Institute of Chicago, the Summer Leadership Institute on Community Economic Development at Harvard Divinity School, and the Information and Services Clearinghouse of the Howard University School of Divinity.

I began this book by describing my vision of the public theolo-gian and pastor as one standing in a particular Christian tradition but speaking to all rational people. I admit my debt to professors and conversation partners at the University of Chicago during the 1970s and 1980s who were occupied with the question of the pub-lic role of religion, and who accepted my argument that, historical-ly, African American leaders like Du Bois and King assumed that personal renewal and social change were an inseparable enterprise. I believe that the renewal of religious congregations, particularly black churches, depends on their ability to retrieve this tradition of public ministry.

In the years ahead, I intend to work on the following dimen-sions of the renewal in public theology and ministry. First, I would like American seminaries to build churches' capacity to engage in comprehensive community development. Professors of social ethics, church and society, practical theology, and field education may be natural resources for initiating this work. However, they must be in conversation and partnership with colleagues in biblical, historical, and systematic theological studies to ensure that the church's ministry evolves in dialectical relationship to Christian tradition and to contemporary realities.

Seminaries should contact community-development professionals in their area to explore possibilities for training clergy in assessing community needs and for mobilizing congregational resources on behalf of the poor. There are several national organizations that could serve as useful resources, including the National Congress of Community Economic Development in Washington, the National Federation of Community Development Credit Unions in New York, and the Local Initiative Support Corporation, which has regional offices throughout the nation.

Second, I think that churches should immediately attend to their support and services for so-called at-risk adolescents. In view of the discussion in chapter 4 regarding the "coming storm" of juvenile violent crime, churches need to determine what role they will play in the lives of the prodigal sons and daughters of the future. Churches must ask what would have happened to the prodigal son in Luke if there had been no father and no open door to which he could have returned. This is a chilling prospect to raise regarding a biblical text in which a supportive family network is in place. For in so many of our communities there is no daddy and no open door. Churches can supply surrogate parents and support systems to insure that youths who want to reform their lives—who want to go home—have someplace to go.

Most churches have not taken ministries for children and youth seriously. That practice must change. As churches retool youth ministries, they should draw on the expertise in the Boys and Girls Clubs, YMCA, YWCA, and in scouting. These agencies have much to teach if churches ask to learn. Drs. Edward and Anne Wimberly, who teach at ITC, have developed one of the more innovative and effective programs for training Christian educators in the educators' own development of ideas to help children and families. Their program should be studied by interested church workers. The Hampton University Ministers Conference has added an annual Christian Educators Conference, which may be the most significant ecumenical gathering of African American Christian educators in the nation.

Third, churches need to improve and expand their use of the media, especially radio and television. Although print media is valuable, it appears that radio and television reach larger segments of the population. My hope is that churches of a variety of theological and political perspectives will enter the marketplace of ideas. It is not useful or accurate to allow the public to conclude that all Christians embrace the theology and politics of a few conservative leaders. There has always been an enormous variety of perspectives within the church, and this variety should be evident on television and radio.

Seminaries should consider presenting mini-courses through televised and broadcast media. This would add to the intellectual capital of congregations while modeling tolerance, open-mindedness, and diversity to a cynical and searching public. As the great theologian and African bishop Augustine said of theological debate and conflict, "In all things that are essential to the faith let there be unity, in all things nonessential, liberty, but in all things, charity."

The call to action has sounded. Government agencies are calling for partners in social service delivery; nonprofit agencies are calling for greater collaboration among community-based organizations; the neediest individuals and families are calling for training, assistance, and care. People of faith now have an opportunity to answer the call, to become agents of community building and development. I have tried to offer vision and practical resources to help the church achieve a more vigorous public witness. It is an exciting time to be alive and working to uplift humanity. It is time to remember the words of the rabbi: "The world is equally balanced between good and evil; your next act will tip the scale."

NOTES

1. Beginnings:
The Making of a Public Theologian

1. Benjamin E. Mays, *Born to Rebel* (New York: Charles Scribner's Sons, 1971), 134.

2. Safe Havens:
The Culture of Black Congregations

1. Molefi Asante, *The Afrocentric Idea* (Philadelphia: Temple University Press, 1987), 92.

2. Jawanza Kunjufu, *Countering the Conspiracy to Destroy Black Boys* (Chicago: African American Images, 1990), 48.

3. Lawrence W. Levine, *Black Culture and Black Consciousness* (Oxford: Oxford University Press, 1977), 32, quoting Mircea Eliade, *The Sacred and the Profane* (New York: Harcourt Brace, 1959).

4. Zora Neale Hurston, *Jonah's Gourd Vine* (New York: Harper & Row, 1934), 175ff.

5. Hortense Spillers, "Martin Luther King, Jr., and the Style of the Black Ser-

mon," in *The Black Experience in Religion*, ed. C. Eric Lincoln (Garden City, N.Y.: Anchor Books, 1971), 77.

6. Martin Luther King, Jr., "Address at Mass Meeting," 5 December 1955, sound recording in the archives of the Martin Luther King Jr. Center for Nonviolent Social Change, Atlanta.

7. For an excellent treatment of spirituality in the African American community see Michael I. N. Dash, Jonathan Jackson, and Stephen C. Rasor, *Hidden Wholeness: An African American Spirituality for Individuals and Communities* (Cleveland: United Church Press, 1997).

3. The Tempest:
The Black Church since the Civil Rights Movement

1. W. E. B. Du Bois, *The Souls of Black Folk* (New York: New American Library, 1969), 54.

2. Vashti McKenzie, *Not Without a Struggle: Leadership Development for African American Women in Ministry* (Cleveland: United Church Press, 1996).

3. American Academy of Homiletics newsletter, Fall 1985.

4. For a useful collection of sermons from the African American Christian pulpit, see J. Alfred Smith, Sr., Walter B. Hoard, and Milton E. Owens, Jr., eds., *Outstanding Black Sermons*, 3 vols. (Valley Forge, Pa.: Judson Press, 1976–82). For sermons by African American women see Ella Pearson Mitchell, ed., *Those Preaching Women: Sermons By Black Women Preachers* (Valley Forge, Pa.: Judson Press, 1983).

5. Cyprian Davis, O.S.B., *The History of Black Catholics in the United States* (New York: Crossroad, 1990), 260.

6. Related to these views, the Congress of National Black Churches in collaboration with the National Coalition of Black Voter Participation in Washington is currently training clergy to organize nonpartisan projects in voter education and policy analysis.

4. Exodus and Return:
Redeeming Prodigal Youths

1. Jacob V. Lamar, Jr., et al., "Today's Native Sons," *Time*, 1 December 1986, 26–29.

2. Dr. Joseph N. Gayles, Jr., quoted in Ann Hardie, "Problems Facing Black Men Threaten U.S. Society, Psychologists Say," *Atlanta Journal-Constitution*, 15 August 1986, sec. D.

3. William J. Bennett, John J. DiIulio, Jr., and John P. Walters, *Body Count: Moral Poverty . . . and How to Win America's War against Crime and Drugs* (New York: Simon & Schuster, 1996).

4. Ibid., 26.

5. Ibid., 27.

6. Mary Shelley, *Frankenstein* (Philadelphia: Courage Books, 1987; original, 1831), 104.

7. William Julius Wilson, *The Truly Disadvantaged* (Chicago: University of Chicago Press, 1987), 13 (emphasis mine).

8. Urban Institute, "Nurturing Young Black Males: Challenges to Agencies, Programs, and Special Policy," ed. Ronald B. Mincy (Washington, D. C., 1994).

9. Joy G. Dryfoos, *Adolescents at Risk: Prevalence and Prevention* (New York: Oxford University Press, 1990),

5. Resources for the Long Haul:
Public-Spirited Partnerships

1. Larry Witham, "Faiths Feel Role Is Tiny at Summit," *Washington Times*, 26 April 1997, sec. A, p. 4.

2. Fred Kammer, S.J., speech at the annual meeting of Volunteers of America, 16 June 1997.

3. Mahatma Gandhi, quoted in Jim Wallis, "Where Do We Go from Philadelphia?" unpublished paper, 1997.

4. W. E. B. Du Bois, *The Seventh Son: The Thought and Writings of W. E. B. Du Bois*, ed. Julius Lester, vol. 1 (New York: Random House, 1971), 575.

6. Vision for the Journey:
New Ministers for Renewed Congregations

1. James MacGregor Burns, *Leadership* (New York: Harper & Row, 1978), 18, 19, 20, 36.

INDEX

93516